From Institutions to

On Becoming Person-Centred

An anthology of selected writings, conversations and interviews by, for and about people with intellectual disabilities and those who care about them.

Edited by Aaron Johannes.
With Patrick McDonagh, Susan Stanfield
and Jim Reynolds

Spectrum Press
A DIVISION OF SPECTRUM SOCIETY

Spectrum Press, Vancouver, 2012 All rights reserved

ISBN: 978-1-105-98972-8

Spectrum Press
A DIVISION OF SPECTRUM SOCIETY

Spectrum Press is a social enterprise operated with, by and for people with disabilities and those who care about them. All profits fund individualised supports furthering literacy, story-telling and self advocate leadership.

Cover illustration: Aaron Johannes "Addicted to the Boat"
www.imagineacircle.com

Index

"The past isn't dead. It isn't even past."
William Faulkner

"...sharing these stories ...enlivens the possibility
for full contributing lives for citizens of all ages
everywhere. As humans, we have been
sharing stories since the dawn of time.
It is time to remember how to share
our stories around the campfires of our lives."
Jack Pearpoint

"People are trapped in history,
and history is trapped in them."
James Baldwin

Introduction:
Are We There Yet?

Aaron Johannes

"All men dream, but not equally. Those who dream by night in the dusty recesses of their minds, wake in the day to find that it was vanity: but the dreamers of the day are dangerous men, for they may act on their dreams with open eyes, to make them possible."
Thomas Edward Lawrence (of Arabia)

It has been a pleasure to go through so many articles, interviews and papers to find those speaking to our theme, which is not merely to provide a context for how people with intellectual disabilities were institutionalised and then returned to community, but to examine how this history and these processes, in the absence of reflection, can continue to inform and even disrupt our contemporary agenda of interdependence through support practices. To this end we wanted to create a kind of kaleidoscopic primer of voices from all corners of our community.

"The Powell River Conversation" was an attempt to bring together such voices, when we first started to think of this anthology; it was an amazing day for all of us, and reinforced that we were on the right track. That event, transcribed and edited, is a kind of conversational backbone to this anthology, with other voices adding to the conversation ...telling stories around the campfire that David imagines. We hope you will join us and add your own stories which, as Jack Pearpoint says, will enliven "the possibility of full contributing lives." Such stories do exist and, told, they have the power to radicalize through an "if/then" paradigm – if this is possible for that person, why not this person? If this is possible for one person, or some people, why not all people? Why not indeed?

As newly adoptive parents we delighted in everything parental, including things that made other parents crazy! Our new son was three years old and an hour into an eight day drive from the west coast to the east when he asked for the first time, "Are we there yet?" When he was little, I would try to predict when he was about to ask, and then before he could say it, I'd ask, "Are we there yet?" to make it his job to answer (there were dire predictions about his ability to speak …he's currently practicing his Shakespeare in hopes of playing Lysander). And he would say, yes, no, or maybe. If he said "Yes," no matter where we were, I'd pull over if I could and say, "Well, here we are!" And sometimes it would be somewhere nifty, like a playground with a fountain on a hot day and we'd have a great time and he would say, "I *knew* we were *here!*" Other times we'd be in the middle of nowhere and I'd stop and say, "Here we are!" and he'd say, "No! This isn't it!" It became a kind of a mantra that plays in my head even as he's moved on into teenage-hood.

There are some corollaries in our field of disability supports. We can easily go from thinking, "Yes, we've made it! We are *here!*" to complete certainty that "We're not there yet." The "not there" is often clear – a group home built for five a quarter century ago, staffed by uniformed people who have little or no values-based training or opportunity for discussion in a town where parents are told that this is just how things are, and no one has looked beyond the horizon. Not there yet! A school with a too well-used resource room – not there yet!   Other times, it is more subtle and we can even feel these things in the same home, with the same person, changing from hour to hour depending on who the person is supported by or spending time with.

How to reflect on such things in a world where we're constantly distracted by the next budget cut, the next new thing, the next memo from above, the next funding formula, the next petition, the next strike threat, the next form that needs filling out. As Norman Kunc and Emma Van der Klift, masters of the metaphor, have said of leadership in our field, our hasty temptation is always to start looking for our lost keys under the street lamp, even though in our hearts we know they went missing in the field, or on the beach, where it is now dark and finding them will be so much harder. We'll need a flashlight and patience and a network of allies. We'll need to admit that it's hard and we're fallible and always learning.

And, indeed, it is hard at every level of caring to keep the person we support front and centre, and even harder to remember to stop and listen and dream together, where the keys are. And yet it does happen. It happens more often when we are with people with disabilities, who often have, among their gifts, the gift of slowing us down so that we can move beyond this constant bubbling turmoil into a state of calm reflection ...

Part of the pleasure of editing this anthology is the richness of materials now available to us. There have never been more successes and they've never been better documented and the documents have never been more available. However, many are only available in places outside the range of our daily services. Part of our intention in this anthology is to bring these worlds of research and practice closer. To host, in effect, a party of friends from all different parts of our lives, with all kinds of different challenges and gifts and experience ...just as many of us already do, in our real inclusive and interdependent lives.

For me, as a parent and friend to people with disabilities, there is also great pleasure in the carefulness with which the authors and interviewees speak of their subject – of people they care about, who are part of their lives, people they *know*.

I always find myself influenced by my history with families who have taught us so much. In a complicated negotiation, with many players and stacks of spreadsheets and a plethora of mounting concerns, all of which I felt I was juggling very professionally and skillfully, the dad leaned over: "Do you like my kid? Do you care about her?" And I thought she was delightful and was really looking forward to her being part of what we make together, so I said so. He nodded. "Then we can figure out everything else," he said. And we did.

So I found myself reading and re-reading prospective articles for this anthology with this simple idea in mind: do you like my kid? Are we there yet? While these are indeed experts, some of them world-renowned in their fields, they are also friends, family and allies to people with disabilities. In a wonderful oral history by Chester Finn, on the Berkeley Library site, Finn talks about the importance of meeting other civic and governmental leaders and getting to know them, because once they know self advocates, they "can't help but want to assist us." Peter Park in his interview says something like, "we have some friends now and that's a step in the right direction." This de-mystification leads to relationship leads to community building leads to political will and advocacy and citizenship – it is a pattern we can see at every level of government and service provision.

We have included here the voices of parents and self advocates. However, increasingly, these distinctions blur as parents move into academia or academics claim, with pride, family members with disabilities, and self advocates go off to university. Disability studies are necessarily interdisciplinary but also increasingly inclusive. Further, we are learning that emancipatory research can be a contribution to a more holistic knowing that can meaningfully impact on how supports are imagined and delivered.

While their disability label may be the first thing we notice about someone when we meet them, it can become the last thing we think of as they become vital parts of our own networks of support and we become part of theirs. It is important to the organization I am part of that there be alternatives to the medicalised model which affects, indeed infects, so many of our culture's assumptions, very often so unnecessarily in the case of people with disabilities, who are not "sick" but incorporate diverse abilities and challenges. The struggle is that we continue to work within a historic paradigm of groups identified, diagnosed, segregated and then disenfranchised.... [1]

---

[1] To find out more about how this works sociologically, check out the excellent new book, *Good Blood, Bad Blood: Science, Nature, and the Myth of the Kallikaks*, by J. David Smith and Michael L. Wehmeyer. Like an unfolding mystery novel, the authors recount how a group of individuals were cut away from the herd, demonized, ridiculed and then used as an example for the eugenicist's cause. Another excellent resource is the essay, "Wife Rena Teary," by Rena Miller, found in Research as *Resistance: Critical, Indigenous and Anti-oppressive Approaches,*

Michael Kendrick has said that all actions proceed out of theory, acknowledged or unacknowledged. It is not until we've identified an alternative place to stand, a different theory, that we can begin to know for certain what we stand for, and what we won't stand for. In our field, it can be the case that what matters is *who* we stand with. In this knowing we can move away from searching in the light of the street lamp for keys into braver searches.

What I have come to believe is most important – and perhaps this makes me see it increasingly in the work of others – is that our neighbourhoods, workplaces, communities and our homes are impoverished by the lack of those we care about, who happen to have intellectual disabilities, as we are diminished by their absence. Recently I spent three weeks in another country in situations that didn't include people with disabilities. The kinds of things that I did there were not so different from what I do here, but there seemed to be no people with disabilities there. I assumed that, as in my home province, they would be present everywhere I went. But they were "not there yet."

This absence became a kind of ringing silence around us, growing daily, which I assumed was just an issue for me, until at the theatre two young ladies with Down Syndrome sat in front of us and I heard my son whisper, "Finally!" In this absence of people with intellectual disabilities, this silence, we might remember the words of poet Adrienne Riche:

> Silence can be a plan rigorously executed
> the blueprint to a life
> It is a presence it has a history   a form
> Do not confuse it with any kind of absence

Parents, self advocates and friends are often faced with this "blueprint," and part of how it is "rigorously executed" is that it

Edited by Leslie Brown and Susan Strega. I think everyone in any "helping profession" should read this essay.
AJ

becomes systemic until we are socialized into a kind of compliance. We're faced with the evident construction and forget that it is all based on a blueprint.

One of the most transformational experiences for me was being asked, in my professional role, to attend a meeting about a child with autism at a local specialist hospital. I was welcomed to an empty seat on one side of the table – I didn't even notice where – and the whole team of professionals, who had been very much stuck in trying to support the challenges of the child and their family, wrote down everything I said, asked me questions, turned my ideas into plans and thanked me profusely for attending. At the end, the family took me aside to say that it was the first time anyone had made sense of their situation.

The next day, as it happened, we had a meeting for our own child in the same place, with many of the same professionals. I found it odd that we were kept waiting in the vestibule – perhaps there was an emergency? And we could see the professionals through the glass doors. We began to wonder with increasing discomfort if they'd forgotten us, and were finally waved into waiting seats on the other side of the table, and they began to make pronouncements about our child that were obviously the result of the discussion about us they'd had while we waited. They'd figured it all out...

A relatively new parent, I missed several cues which I now know (and can ignore, knowingly) as I was not socialized to pick up on through endless meetings that begin right after birth. Compliance is not really my nature, but it might have been more likely. Instead, I was excited to be problem solving about ways to expand his possibilities and keep him healthy, strong and ambitious. I was excited to be with professionals who had been such attentive listeners the day before, when we were all equal. I was engaged in what I expected to be a productive, helpful conversation. However, I began to sense increasing discomfort from the other side of the table as my partner and I batted their ideas around and tested them to see what held water. Finally the psychologist, in frustration, said, "But you don't understand – WE are the professionals; you know your child; WE know hundreds of children with this diagnostic picture; you know what his teacher says and she is comparing him to 30 or 60 or 90 children; WE know the findings of research from around the world about children who have this diagnosis." Every time she said "WE" she indicated her side of the table by waving her hands. Every time she said "you" she pointed to our side of the table.

As in one of our most traditional and failure-ridden educational models, a model that works least well for adults and does not work at all for those who have pre-knowledge about the subject area, we were to have entered the room *tabula rasa*, empty and unquestioning vessels to be filled with their expertise. On the one hand, it was a horrific experience (and one more common for families than anyone would imagine). On the other hand, it was great to have it so baldly stated. The people I thought were here to help were firmly situated on the other side of that table. The table was, as much as the walls of the institutions, which we have so carefully closed, an "othering" force. As Lyle Romer says, "When the institutions were open, at least we knew where they were." This differentiation and othering based on a lens of needs, created by a professional body that feels unanswerable, can leave one feeling quite alone and quite mad. Years of it can cause, some experts suggest, a kind of post traumatic stress disorder. Certainly I know more than a few parents who start to tremble and hyper-ventilate at the thought of a being called into a meeting.

Yet, you would not believe, out of that deftly differentiating hand wave that "othered" us as parents, what trouble I've caused since! And I am hardly alone, but one of many parents who have been subject to these forces and decided to follow a different path that led to more fitting goals. In such moments are we radicalized and then compelled to talk and gather in force and write and publish.

Yet this experience of professionals (and what might be called pseudo-professionals or proto-professionals) is often unrecognized by them. A friend recently posted on Facebook a funny and sad animated video about a mother's experience of a transition planning meeting with professionals, for her son. It was haunting, as when you suddenly realize a joke encapsulates your own experience. Ouch. What was interesting was that in her wide range of friends the teachers, behaviour consultants and social workers all commented, "I hope I never work there!" and "That's certainly not how *we* do it," while the parents all unequivocally agreed it reflected their actual experience. Unequivocally. Not a single parent saying, "Oh that wasn't my experience at all." Not a single professional said, "I must change my ways" or even "We must remember this is the experience that people have had before they come to us."

Soon after this a friend of a friend, a teacher, ended up on my own Facebook page, objecting to something that I'd posted. As much as I rationally explained that I'd posted this with some thought and that it represented the experience of many people with disabilities, and that I felt her response to it was dismissive of my own life experience and that of many parents, she continued to respond that I was wrong. We were wrong. Teachers would never do such things. Teachers do such things, I said, and gave her examples. You are dismissing my experience. Teachers have done more for people with disabilities than anyone else in history, she said. This is only resoundingly indicative of someone who has not read history.

It reminded me of the guestbook to the Michael de Courcey photographic installation, "Asylum: a long last look at Woodlands, 1878 to 2003," which documented the closure of our last major institution by interviewing and photographing people who had moved into their own homes in their communities. In the guestbook those who had worked at the institution, one of the largest employers in the small city of New Westminster, had written wonderful memories of eating warm baked cookies in the kitchens, sleigh rides in the snow, summer picnics and "family" festivals (all for staff) on the grounds. Often they wrote intergenerationally: their grandparents, parents and then they themselves worked there and were part of that community. And between these reminiscences those who had actually lived there scrawled things like, "I hope it burns to the ground!" "It was hell." "I would die before I returned." Out of such professionalized "othering" comes the ability to completely ignore what was written, literally, between the lines, but hardly covertly. This huge, unrecognized communication gap between the two, even as they interacted at the same gallery opening, and even as mutual friends on Facebook, will continue as long as we don't stop to reflect on this powerful and often unconsidered medicalised model.

Yet, as soon as we recognise it exists we can find immediate opportunities to be vigilant about its manifestations. We can refuse to be prey to its hydra-headed influences, as families, as individuals, as organizations and as agencies.

For those of us who support families, however, I want to suggest that we have an added responsibility to think critically and reflect. Families are often least equipped for this battle – most of us have no idea what we're getting into when we have a child with a disability.

With almost twenty years as a professional in the field of disability supports, a renowned advocate and authority in my area, I was taken aback almost from the first moment after signing the adoption papers by assumptions that immediately came into play. We were blamed for things we hadn't even been present for, having adopted a toddler. Pat Fratangelo has said that it is not a matter of whether or not we engage in this othering process, it's of how we each engage (or are disenfranchised) in subtle ways and how we can each refuse to participate in anything less that inclusive communities of valued members of all kinds. As professionals we can insist on round tables and discourses between equals. We can refuse to use acronyms. We can take notes and refer to them so that families and self advocates don't need to repeat the same information to exhaustion. We can use graphics when we're supporting someone who doesn't read. We can admit that we don't know everything. We can ask to join in the search for what would be "optimal" for the individual rather than focusing on which of our three "program" choices might be least objectionable. We can, most of all, continue to learn to listen better and more deeply. We can, as David Pitonyak says, let the moms and dads be moms and dads. We can, as parent Erin Sheldon does in her contribution, continue to remind those around us about the gifts our children bring to places that are owned by the community they are part of.

Through the process of editing this book I have been reminded of thriller movies in which the protagonist steadfastly refuses to turn around, fearing that the monster is right behind, and then, unable to bear the tension, finally does turn, and finds what many of these authors have found: the monster is not behind them after all, yet when they turn to move forward again, there it is right in front of them.

This still felt shadow of an institution as monster is clear in the literature of self advocates and families. It is an axiom of our field that these are almost always the leaders in our thinking. Yet the literature of operationalizing community living as a thing distinct from institutions rarely has much to say about our history. Indeed, perhaps our most important historical document, Burton Blatt and Fred Kaplan's *Christmas In Purgatory: A Photographic Essay On Mental Retardation,* published in 1966, is currently out of print (though now available online) and we routinely speak to rooms of a hundred people of whom only a few know what normalization is and who Wolf Wolfensberger, the father of de-institutionalisation, was and why he matters. We end up in heart-breaking situations like that at a conference I attended, in which Fred Ford gave a great presentation on the history of people with disabilities and self advocacy and one of the elders stood up, so excited, gave a great fist pump and said, "I had no idea we had a history! This is all making sense now!" Indeed.

We are extremely lucky in Canada that the People First movement has been such a strong influence on our culture and, in British Columbia, that so many strong families have so unequivocally stated what they need and want for their children. It is these folks, self advocates and families, who led us to close all our provincial institutions and insist on increasingly integrated services. If we look through our history, it was never the government, the unions, the service organizations, the schools, the advocates or the professionals who led the way to the changed society which those of us who include people with disabilities in our lives in vital ways are excited about.

And yet, now, we are at something of a confused moment in time. People use the same language to describe very different ideas. Great concepts have been co-opted. In a state in the U.S. where institutions continue, lobbyists insist that if people with disabilities are to have a full range of choices, they must continue to be allowed to live in institutions and attend sheltered day programs. In our own province "community living" can mean that you are kept in a home in a neighbourhood where there are institutional signs on the walls and the staff wear uniforms and eat in the staff room, before or after you eat, or you can be supported in your own home by people you consider to be friends, who you have selected to spend time with.

We've heard of "positive behavioural support" being used to describe situations in which restraints were used; of "shared living" describing situations in which the living was not at all shared – the person with the disability in the basement had their food delivered to their door, or there were five people living in one home with workers coming in and out to "share" their living; we've seen "group homes" that were nothing like a "home"; we've seen "person centred planning" in which the "dreams" of the person consisted of extinguishing his 8 challenging behaviours; we've seen "inclusive" classrooms in which the children with disabilities were included in the day's opening and then shuffled off to the resource room. In none of this can we begin to have useful conversations until we know where we stand and out of what philosophy we're working.

It is with the furtherance of such questioning in mind that these essays and interviews have been collected. Someone once said something like, "just when you think you have the answers, the questions change." In the field of community support, we had only just figured out really great answers about how to run really great group homes and segregated centres and sheltered workshops and then the questions changed, the definitions changed and the expectations of those we support and those who care about them changed. Now is the time for some new questions.

Perhaps we have never been better poised for better questions and processes through which dialogue can be generated. The wonderful grass roots advocacy movement of the 70s and 80s seems to be in resurgence and people like John O'Brien, Connie Lyle O'Brien, Emma Van der Klift and Norman Kunc continue to be active and wonderfully engaged and engaging. Leaders like David Pitonyak and Michael Kendrick have only become clearer in their ideas as they travel the world and amass endless experiences of actual lives and supports. All of this is augmented by a new interdisciplinary academic field out of which a new crop of authorities such as Tanya Titchkosky, Dan Goodley, Jan Walmsley and B.C.'s own Tim Stainton are creating new, deeper conversations informed by new research, often in liaison with research partners with intellectual disabilities.

More and more, people with disabilities are part of such conversations, and an increasing number of parents have gone on to reflective careers as teaching advocates, sharing not just their research but their experiences. We can look at the oral histories of leaders such as Chester Finn and Linda Kunick and Paul Young and Peter Park. For the first time, thanks not least to Christopher Goodey and Patrick McDonagh, we have marvelous histories of disability as concept and sociological phenomenon. We are more connected internationally than ever before, allowing for an exchange of ideas that is unprecedented – the Belgian writer Dr. Griet Roets, has been one of my largest influences and I have almost instantaneous access to her published work, whereas per-internet I'd have had to wait years. We have, thanks to leaders like Margaret Wheatley, John McKnight, Peter Block, Juanita Brown and David Isaacs, new ways of having "conversations that matter," based on invitation, better listening, shared leadership and open-ness to diversity. Perhaps best of all, we have amassed multitudinous experience of multiple lives lived well, in which the gifts of people with disabilities have been shared widely, to the betterment of their communities and networks. We have success stories. *We know how to do it.* A different path is clearly marked – we only have to decide to go there.

However, almost as if in reaction to all of this, there is a concurrent upsurge in conservative ideologies and practices: agencies that are increasingly entrenched; parent driven groups that call for further layers of monitoring and "social work" practices; new and formulaic practices in which lives are dissected, deconstructed, judged and re-scripted; the kinds of accreditation practices which did so little good in institutions are moving into the community and taking up time, energy and funding; a whole new crop of acronyms and pseudo-professionalized practices. Clay Shirky, in a TED talk "Institutions versus Collaboration" says that what institutions go through when they are told they are unnecessary is akin to Elizabeth Kubler-Ross's stages of grief: denial, anger, bargaining, depression, acceptance. Look at the media reports in your area and you are likely to find evidence of this.

The movement from institutions to individualization is a complicated one as it is part of a civil rights movement that depends, as no other social justice movement has, on the support of allies and partners. Given this, as allies let us not be distracted from reflection which clarifies our own ideas and ideals, and then move ever forward, with our friends and neighbours, until we are, all of us, *there*.

From Institutions to Individuals:
On Becoming Person-Centred

Susan Stanfield

When we hear the word *institution* in the context of community living, we think of the daunting, prison-like structures where people with disabilities were warehoused through much of the last century. The very term "community living" denotes a position against such structures and the exclusionary attitudes that led to their creation. But institutions aren't just a physical thing. The word also applies to organizations (as in a banking institution, or educational institution), and to social customs (the institution of marriage). To be "institutional" is to be structured, formalized, bound by a set of established principles or rules. A *system* can be institutional, through its policies and practices, without any physical manifestation of what we commonly think of as an institution.

The service delivery system for people with developmental disabilities is in many ways an institutional system. It's structured, formalized, bound by rules...and while we're starting to move toward more individualized options, many of the existing services still operate within an institutional framework. The overwhelming majority of funding is allocated to agencies that deliver services to groups of people in the form of programs – residential programs, day programs, supported work programs. The stated mandate of such programs is to help people become more independent and more included in the community, but the assumption that a *program* is the means to that end represents an institutional way of thinking; a way of thinking that lingers with us from a past we're still working to overcome. We closed the big institutions, but, in some cases, replaced them with new structures that are every bit as rigid and inflexible.

We're just now starting to realize the limitations of some of our program models. They're expensive to operate, difficult to change, constrained by bureaucracies and hierarchies that often place more value on the input of professionals and program supervisors than that of individuals and families – even to the point of sustaining a particular model past the point when it ceases to be relevant. How does an agency that only runs congregated group activity programs respond to a new generation of youth who don't want day programs?

Over the past decade, service providers have begun

downsizing their large facility-based programs, in what feels like a case of déjà vu for anyone who was part of the institutional downsizing projects. But it's important to keep in mind that size alone isn't the issue: to change the appearance but not the fundamental approach to supporting people will only perpetuate the institutional system. The shift away from large group settings to smaller, more normalized environments is a positive one, for sure – but this shift must be accompanied by a whole new approach, one that genuinely supports (rather than directs) individuals and families, that builds flexible supports around individuals instead of forcing them to fit into pre-defined *placements.*

Toward a person-centred approach

In recent years, the term *person-centred* has made its way into human services vernacular. The term was popularized by Psychologist Carl Rogers in the 1950s to describe a therapeutic approach that recognized the patient's innate motivation to develop his or her potential to the fullest extent possible. According to Rogers, the role of the therapist was to create an environment where his patients felt safe and supported to explore their potential; it was not the therapist's job to solve people's problems or dictate a course of action. Rogers' approach was "nondirective" – meaning the therapist was there to nurture the person's natural curiosity and desire for self actualization, not to *fix* people. Fundamental to his approach was the belief that people have the capacity to solve their own problems, given appropriate support, and that *relationships* are key to our personal growth and development.

It's a pretty simple idea, really. Unfortunately, we have a tendency in our field to take simple ideas and make them complicated – to institutionalize them. By definition, person-centredness is about individuals; it's not about systems and structures. It doesn't lend itself to standardization. It's not a bureaucratic exercise we go through once a year as part of a mandated planning meeting. We must take care not to institutionalize this idea, to turn it into another task that gets added to the endless "to do" list (replace *the furnace filter....tally the petty cash...do the person-centred planning...).*

It's easy for organizations to claim they're being person-centred, but the evidence doesn't always bear out the claim. Taking groups of people on outings of the staff's choosing in a 12-passenger van is not person-centred. Renting a bigger space so the day program can accommodate more people is not person-centred. Replacing swimming with arts and crafts because the new staff doesn't know how to swim (but loves doing arts and crafts) is not person-centred. Hiring staff without the input of those they'll be supporting is not person-centred. Providing everyone's support from 9-3, Monday through Friday, because that's when the program operates, is not person-centred.

And yet all of these things happen in the current service system. We're so used to doing things a certain way that we often don't notice the extent to which our structures are limiting people until someone from outside the system points it out. A new support worker asks, "Why *don't I meet Charlie at his house at 9:00 and go straight from there to his volunteer job?*" and we suddenly realize we've been making Charlie come all the way across town to our program site just to meet up with a staff person, turn around, and go back across town to his volunteer job.

Or in another example, a group of participants who might be capable of taking transit use the program's passenger van, because it's there. Or a young woman who may only need a few hours of support has staff with her 24 hours a day, because that's how the group home is staffed. A kind of "regression to the mean" occurs, where the diversity of individual strengths and capabilities becomes increasingly uniform – noone's needs are entirely satisfied, but everyone is somewhat satisfied. We settle for the lowest common denominator, for passive participation over active engagement: watching movies, listening to music, being taken on van outings, having meals prepared and served by staff. At best, this one-size-fits-all approach keeps people entertained and cared for; at worst, it instills in them a sense of learned helplessness. The person's pre-supposed need for constant staff support becomes a self fulfilling prophesy.

So, what does it mean to be person-centred? For starters, it means checking our impulse to jump in and take charge of people's lives. It means resisting the temptation to group people on the basis of disability. Perhaps most importantly, it means involving the right people in decision-making – families, friends, significant others – and not presuming that we have all the answers. It's not enough to invite families to a meeting, present them with a plan we've come up with, and ask them after the fact if they have anything else to contribute. Being person-centred requires that we get to know the person and those closest to them at a whole different level from what we're used to, and that we actively encourage and support their involvement in the planning process:

• **Who is in the person's life?** Who helps the person make decisions, who do they enjoy spending time with? What role do family members have? Are there siblings, grandparents, family friends who might like to be more involved? It's important to get clear on who is part of the person's existing and potential network, so we can support the *network,* not just the individual. We can't (and shouldn't) do everything ourselves.

• **How and where does the person like to spend their time?** What are the *natural supports* (the people and resources that are available to everyone) that might be tapped in some of those environments?

• **What, specifically, does the person need support with?** Think in terms of targeted support, as opposed to coverage. *"How many hours of staffing do you need?"* leads to one kind of discussion; *"What are your goals, and how can we support you to achieve them?"* leads to a whole other discussion.

• **Who might provide the needed support?** We sometimes assume that whatever support someone needs, our staff will provide it. A good rule of thumb is to ask ourselves, if we needed support with the same activity, who would we turn to? Look *first* at natural supports you might access or enlist. If the person needs transportation to work, is there a co-worker they might car-pool with?

Starting with these questions can lead to a whole different plan than we're likely to come up with on our own. But the plan is just the beginning. Being person-centred doesn't end with a good plan. It's a way of *being* in our relationship to those we support. It's a journey we take together, as equals. It requires tremendous organizational support, a genuine letting go of some of our power and control.

The chart below examines some of the differences between a *program* approach and a *person-centred* approach:

In a program...	In a person-centred service...
Decision making is driven by staff and professionals	Decision making is driven by the individual and his/her support network
Planning occurs as a singular event, according to a prescribed format	Planning is ongoing and individualized
The person's goals are defined within the context of the program	The person's goals are defined within the context of a holistic plan
Specialized supports are the first response to meeting individual needs	Generic supports are the first response
Staff take the place of natural supports	Staff augment natural supports
There is a pre-set schedule of activities that people take part in (or don't)	Individuals develop their own personal schedule based on their goals
Staffing is provided at pre-set times according to a fixed schedule	Staffing is provided flexibly
Focus on participation Focus on group needs	Focus on increased independence Focus on individual needs
Staff skills determine the selection of activities	Preferred activities inform the selection of staff with appropriate skills
Support is tied to the program – the person can't take their support with them if they leave	Services are portable – the person can take their support and change service providers if

the program	they so choose

A tale of two approaches

To illustrate how these two approaches might play out in someone's life, consider the case of "Anne":

Anne, a 21-year old woman with a developmental disability, is seeking community support services. She is described as being friendly, outgoing, and having a variety of interests, especially classical music and spending time with children. Her parents are concerned that Anne spends too much of her time at home and, since finishing high school, has lost touch with her social group. She has no close friends.

Approach # 1) ABC Community Services: A program approach

ABC Community Services has a vacancy in its "Friendship Centre" day program, which operates out of its head office. The intake worker feels this program would be a good fit for Anne, so she signs her up and arranges for Anne to be picked up by HandyDart at home each morning. At the centre, Anne takes part in various activities: arts and crafts, exercise class, cooking, karaoke, dancing. On Wednesdays the group goes to an adapted aquatics program at the local pool, and on Fridays they meet up with participants from another day program. Weather permitting, they have a barbecue at the park, but on rainy days they all watch movies at the centre. At her annual planning meeting a year later, Anne says she enjoys the day program but would like to find a part-time job. The program manager tells her the agency's supported employment program doesn't have any vacancies right now but they'll put Anne on the waitlist, and in the meantime they'll request a vocational assessment.

Three years later, Anne is still at the centre. The vocational assessment indicated that Anne needed to learn some pre-employment skills before she'd be ready for the supported employment program, but unfortunately the day program doesn't have enough staff to support her to learn these skills. Anne's parents are still concerned about her social isolation. They feel she is showing signs of depression, and are also concerned that she has picked up some ritualistic behaviors from another participant at the day program. The manager suggests they put in a referral for a behavioral assessment.

Five years later, Anne is still at the Friendship Centre. Her parents are worried about what will become of her when they're no longer able to care for their daughter. ABC Community Services agrees to put her on the waitlist for one of their group homes.

Approach # 2) XYZ Community Services: A person-centred approach

XYZ Community Services spends time getting to know Anne and her family. They ask what kind of a life Anne envisions for herself, what she likes to do, what interests she'd like to develop, who she'd like to spend time with. They learn that Anne has a cousin, Marie, who she used to be very close to. Marie is married now, with two young children, and Anne doesn't get to see her very often because she lives about 50 miles away in another town. They talk about other people who used to be part of Anne's life, and make a list of people Anne would like to follow up with. A support worker helps Anne set up an email account and get in touch with some of her friends from high school through a social networking site. Anne reconnects with her cousin Marie, who is delighted to hear from her. Marie sends Anne some pictures of her children and invites Anne to come visit them sometime. In keeping with Anne's interest in music, her support worker arranges for her to sit in on a symphony rehearsal at the big concert hall downtown, which Anne loves; they go back again, and again, and eventually Anne begins volunteering at the symphony as a greeter.

At a team meeting a year later, Anne talks about the new friends she's made and how she's learned to take the bus independently to her volunteer job at the symphony. She's been to visit her cousin a few times and got tickets for Marie and the kids to a special children's concert at the symphony, which they all enjoyed very much.

Three years later, Anne is working two evenings a week in the gift shop at the symphony. Her volunteer job as a greeter has been expanded to include helping with school tours, where she gets to interact with groups of children. She and Marie get together about once a month, and correspond regularly via email.

Five years later, Anne is living in an apartment with a roommate. She's looking forward to hosting Christmas dinner at her place this year.

ABC Community Services gave Anne a program. XYZ Community Services gave her a good life.

Which would you rather have?

The time is now

Person-centred approaches aren't just the latest trend in social services. They're a natural next step in the evolution of the community living movement. If the goal is to see all people enjoy full citizenship and equality, then we need to recognize the limitations of the current service system. When we group people together on the basis of disability, when we build programs and then populate them with people who fit a certain set of criteria, we perpetuate an institutional way of thinking. Not all people will *fit.* Others will refuse to comply with our rules, and may even be asked to leave. Those who comply will likely stay for a very long time – a lifetime, perhaps.

Spending one's entire adult life in a day program, with no other options from which to make an informed choice, is not full citizenship.

It's time we embrace a new way of thinking about the people who come to us for services, to stop seeing them as *clients in a service delivery system,* and instead see them as *individuals in community.*

Let's put institutional thinking behind us, once and for all.

The Powell River Conversation
September 30, 2011 Part One:
"How much history we hold"

Julia Downs, Maria Glaze,
Aaron Johannes, Norman Kunc,
David Pitonyak, Shelley Nessman,
Jim Reynolds, Susan Stanfield,
Alison Taplay, Emma Van der Klift

As we talked about the focus of this upcoming anthology we became aware that many of those we respect and admire work on their own and don't have the infrastructure of an organization to support them or, as parents, have found themselves thrown unexpectedly into conversations (which they would rather not be having). It will always be hard for them to take time to write. However, we wanted to document a dialogue about changes leading up to our current state and the changes we hope to see. As we continued to dream about possibilities, we wondered what might happen if we brought together a team of parents, instructors, consultants and leaders – for one day, in a place away from all our usual concerns, which has its own long history of inclusion building post-institutionalization, and just opened up a conversation, loosely based on Susan's essay...

Emma: I'm becoming very aware as I look around the room, of how much history we hold. It is astonishing really. And I think we need to find ways to do what you've invited us here to do, to preserve some of that and to think about how things have changed.

Aaron: The interesting thing about this exact moment in our province is that in B.C. a foundational part of our disability history, Woodlands, our largest and oldest provincial institution, will be demolished next week the demolition of the final part of the final building. So there was one big institution, which has been mostly replaced by condominiums, and then there was this one last tower – and discussion about what to do with it. Was it historically important enough to keep as a landmark? Who's history did it represent? And then there was a fire, and it was nearly destroyed and the only part that was left was the central tower. I'm an advisor with B.C. People First and they'd been having a campaign to have it torn down, so next week there's a ceremony and they've invited people who used to live at Woodlands to be part of the ceremony – a kind of final goodbye.

Emma: I was at a workshop years and years and years ago where one of the people who had lived at Woodlands talked about trying to burn it down during her time there. I think she might have started her attempts in the kitchen.

Susan: For so many of the people we knew it was a fantasy – they would describe it in detail, how they'd like to tear it down, and bash it with sledgehammers.... Shortly after the fire there was a big conference and for many of the self advocates who had lived there it was what they wanted to talk about... Fred Ford mentioned something about the fire and the audience erupted in applause.

Aaron: And next week will be the final bit of that dream coming true... what I find interesting in it all is the idea of Foucault, the idea of that tower – moving from the idea that people are in dungeons to the idea that people are seen from the tower, possibly, and that they then become responsible for monitoring themselves and each other ...

Emma: Surveillance!

Norman: Panopticon!

Aaron: Yes, the panopticon – Benthem's[1] idea of how surveillance could be designed that didn't depend on paid overseers, and people could be controlled by each other and eventually just by the possibility of being observed from a tower – and, interestingly, the last part of Woodlands that was there was this tower. So we're no longer keeping people in place, in groups, but they still have the sense they're being watched for "appropriate" behaviour.

I know from talking to you both [Norman and Emma] how important this idea of the panopticon and Foucault's work has been to your thinking – and I always find it fascinating that Foucault's books were one of the first things Spectrum bought for their library.

Shelley: There's an interesting parallel in terms of wanting to turn the tower into something else and how we've taken group homes, which started with the intention of being real homes with shared supports and intentional community, and turned that

---

[1] The concept of the panopticon is written about in Michel Foucault's *Discipline and Punish* and well worth an examination for anyone concerned with how minorities are kept apart as it has great implications for people with disabilities. For example, "The constant division between the normal and the abnormal, to which every individual is subjected ... by applying the binary branding ... [leads to] the existence of the whole set of techniques and institutions for measuring, supervising and correcting the abnormal [which] brings into play the disciplinary mechanisms . . ." AJ

lifestyle into something else.   This twisting of intention runs through so many of our methods ...

Emma: We often blindly run through planning sessions without thinking about how loaded some of the concepts we talk about actually are, how loaded some of the language is – we think we are all on the same page, but we might not be, even though we're using the same words. For example, we talk about "wanting the best" for the people we support. Ask ten people what the best is, and you'll get ten different definitions.

Alison: Isn't that the whole thing about being person-centred though? You have to be individualized and sensitive about how to be person-centred. Whenever you adopt something wonderful like PATHs as the new system; when you say instead of doing ISPS [Individual Service Plans], we're now going to do PATHs - you're already tripping on your own mistake. A PATH can be a really great experience for some people but not everyone. A PATH can be very well facilitated or it can be "implemented." And here's another challenge for person-centered planners. I don't know about you but I'm really private about my life. I have a huge number of friends and acquaintances but a very small group of people who really, really, really, really know what's going on with me. A PATH would be my nightmare – I'd have to lie so that you would finish my PATH without learning more about me than I was comfortable sharing! I'd have to sort of pretend to be not myself in some ways – invent things - nice things - about myself. It's just the truth about who I am – I'm private.

Aaron: But if we played your favourite music and had your favourite food, it would be okay, right?

Alison: And if I could do a collage! Well yeah, then it would all be fine, wouldn't it? (if you have read David Hingsburger you will catch the sarcasm here!)

Aaron: Susan and I, for a while now, have been meeting people who care deeply about the folks with disabilities who bring all of us together, and they are great and creative and wonderful, but they don't seem to have a sense of what's brought us to this place.

They have what seem to them great ideas like, "What if we fund-raise for a great big yellow bus, and then everyone could be having more fun *together*. Then we could *all* go to the community centre... or better yet, rent a bigger room just for them!" And they don't know that exactly that kind of segregation is a big part of our history. As soon as they do they say, "Okay, now I get it; now that it has been put into a different context."

There are also people out there doing amazing things, connecting folks in their communities, and they need to know they are not alone on this path. In some places things are split right down the middle – people who believe in community living as we've known it and people who believe in what they think of as *"the more serious stuff"* – which is often the parts of our field that are about collecting data, creating systems, changing "behaviours" -all the various kinds of dehumanizing activities which avoid the kinds of questioning that humanism depends on. So, in the same home, the "serious" staff with the clipboard counting behaviours gets more kudos than the person who is helping them meet their neighbours and get jobs and be part of a congregation and learn to square dance – working to support people in places and with people with whom they don't have those behaviours. We've seen some pretty dysfunctional situations, in which even the staff who is doing all the connecting and caring has been trained to present that they are dispassionate professionals focused on programs... its easy to get them to tell stories and they remember every birthday and celebration and every tiny little achievement of these people they are so close to, but try to talk to them about how that connection feels and they are convinced they're being accused of being unprofessional.

To put our conversation into some kind of context, we want to be able to give those who are looking for something different, perhaps more humanist, another resource. Susan's essay has been downloaded many times and we've met people from all over who have used it in training, so it seemed like a great place to begin a discussion.

Susan: The core idea in my essay is that institutions are not just places like Woodlands that people think of when they hear the word, but that we have since built this institutional system of services that can be every bit as restrictive and segregated as the big institutions were. Even a one person home can be an institution. So it's not the physical notion of an institution, as much as it is a different way of being with people. That kind of paternalistic approach, as opposed to a more facilitative and inclusive approach.

We get people, parents of 19 or 20 year olds, who are still phoning up and saying, "Okay, we're ready for our group home now. And, of course, we'll need a day program too." They have been supported to believe that that is what the adult system is; that there would be this adult system of services that their adult children would come into and be taken care of. Thirty years ago that was true. In some agencies, it is still true, but that, to us, is part of that institutional mind-set that we are working to move past. And when we talk to those parents, invariably they end up saying, "I had no idea that what you are offering was possible. Of course I'd rather my son or daughter had a home of their own and directed their own life and had friends." But this is often the first time that anyone has talked to them about that.

Julia: It just comes back to me, having a 28 year old, that some of the stuff that happens in the school system really, really needs to be built on; thinking about the idea of a circle of friends, for example. Those connections can be re-established. Now I don't have kids in school, but it seems that all we're hearing about is autism and behaviour management, and segregation within the schools seems to be on the rise.

Susan: It is almost going in the other direction, towards further specialization and further segregation, further *expertise*.

Julia: Families need to be exposed to another viewpoint, so they can at least get some idea of what is possible.

Maria: I have a daughter who will be 28 soon and our roots go back to moving to Calgary so she could attend an early intervention program for children with autism. This was when she was age 2. I was complicit in the torture, and I reflect on that a lot. We've been involved with the Family Support Institute for about 15 years. One of the people that profoundly shook me up in my way of looking at how to support my daughter was you, Norman (Kunc). Some of the things you wrote really made me stop and think. I was pissed off, in a way, because it challenged everything I had been lead to believe. I was the good Mom and did whatever the professionals told me. I was so good – I had several intervention programs going at once. I was washing dishes one day, I remember, and I cut my finger quite badly. I needed stitches, I needed to get to the hospital, but I said, "No, I can't go, I am on a twenty minute toileting program!" It's been a huge journey to get where I am with my daughter now, to get to a place where we can trust the dreams and the hopes we have for her life in this small community (Powell River) - a community that we moved to with the intention to create a life for her that we feel we could slip out of as we get older and die, and it should still be okay.

Aaron: This fascinating cycle of creating agencies to support folks but it seems like increasingly people like your family are returning to places like this, where there's a community that seems to you more reliable than the agencies. It reminds me of how institutions were originally created for the benefit of communities and then community people – families and self advocates – said, no, that's not it, and created the agencies people are now wondering about. I think this is the wondering for all of us, about where we are now, and how we got here.

Alison: I have had my feet firmly planted on this road a long time believing that I could change the system from within, and I have to say, I haven't been successful at doing that. I have had some wonderful opportunities to do some very person-centred things in the 1990's in Port Alberni, where we created some individualized services for people before agencies were mandated to. I think that those situations were well thought out and created with the individual at the center. We had some wonderful results for people. In the last few years I've also had a chance to help people expand their personal networks.

But it was a very uphill battle, because, Aaron, when you were telling the story of including everyone on the big yellow bus, it hit home. Because we would just start doing some solid work helping individuals build a very personal network and the very next thing that happened was that the people in the network wanted to reconnect back with their own community, so they'd say, "We should invite all of the people from the group home into this person's circle because it is so wonderful, and then everyone can share it." Every time we'd have to go back and revisit how that wouldn't really work. It has been quite the journey. My experience learning about network development is only one of the reasons that I think now is an important time to reflect on where we have been and where we are going. We are certainly in this huge flux or change, and not just in community living, but around the globe.

Susan: I worked for the two largest organizations in the province. Ernie Baatz, the other co-founder of Spectrum, and I met through the Autism Society of B.C. doing recreation/summer camp duties. I was volunteer coordinator there for a while and we were both on the board. A lot of the kids from the Autism Society were our age, and it always struck us how different the options were for us and our friends compared to these autistic kids, who had up until then gone through a more or less inclusive education – for the time. But when *they* got out of school, the social worker's transition plan was that there are these two group homes available. Which one do you want to move into? And then here are the choices of sheltered workshops, so pick a spot – and that was it. So, they were expected to pick their group home, pick their day program or sheltered workshop, and that's where they would be forever and ever. So, we had the idea that we would start our own organization. We found out about the institutional downsizing projects. It happened to be the same year that Woodlands was downsizing. Tranquille had already closed. And so that's where we focused our energy for the next ten years. We supported people to move out of Woodlands. Aaron joined us early on. He had also worked at some of the bigger organizations. And so the three of us have grown the organization from just having one group home into something that I don't think any of us would have imagined 25 years ago.

Our innovation around the group homes was, instead of one home for four people, we bought duplexes, so that only two people would have to share the home. We realize now that this was innovative in its day, but it's not any more. We soon realized that people didn't want to stay there forever, and they didn't always get along, or appreciate the staff we were hiring for them. And so it has been incredible learning for us. I guess we're hoping that we're making a change from within the system.

Five years ago, we had no one living in their own place, directing their own support with an unpaid caregiver in a shared living arrangement. As of this year, we'll have more people living in arrangements like that than we have in staffed homes.

We have never had anyone leave a staffed resource and ask to go back. They all prefer living in their own place with people they have chosen to live with who care about them, directing their own services.

Aaron: I often wonder why we didn't think of some of these ideas earlier ...

David: I had this dream once that I woke up from laughing out loud. It occurred to me, in a sleep state, that I actually believed that one day we would create a system that works almost flawlessly *most* of the time. You know, this well-tuned machinery that asks the right questions, delivers the right answers, and assures state-of-the-art services for person after person, year after years. There I was, lying in bed, laughing out loud. Laughing at how silly the idea is and realizing simultaneously that however ridiculous, there was a part of me that believed it could happen. Out of this "waking up" came my presentation, *One Day the World Will Be a Perfect Place: Strategies for the Meantime.*

I have been fascinated ever since I had that dream with the things *outside* of our processes and procedures and interventions that truly make a difference in people's lives. What stands out for me is relationships. When we are connected to people we care about and who care about us, the chances of things going well improve dramatically. We are hard-wired to belong.

Neuroscientists tell us that about 80% of what our brain is up to at any given point in time is processing social relationships. Eighty percent! If we are not focused on a specific task that requires a specific kind of attention, our brains are processing our *social* world 80% of the time. I think that's amazing!

Not surprisingly then, being lonely is not good for human beings. Loneliness is at odds with our basic programming, our biology. Some epidemiologists believe that loneliness is on a par with smoking two packs of cigarettes per day as a hazard to our health. Knowing this, it is not a leap to believe that the root of many people's suffering is loneliness. And I think this is especially true for people who experience disabilities.

That's why I get nervous when people think the solution to our problems is to build better 'systems.' Systems can be odds with the work of helping people develop relationships for tons and tons of reasons, not the least of which is that systems often separate people from their natural communities in the name of 'treatment.'

The story you told, Maria, about how, even with a cut finger, you had to go through this program. However ill-informed those programs might have been, you were not doing it because you meant to bring any harm to your daughter. You adored her and you believed that if you do this then she'd be getting what she needed. It took some time; it took some more information, like Norman's writing and other things, to get you to get unseated from that place. I bet it took a huge network of people to get you from that Mom who can't go to the hospital, to a place where you could calm down and think about things more broadly. So, again, I am really fascinated by the ways in which we do that for each other in 'community'.

In the busy world that is our system, people don't have or take the time to sit down and explore what's going on. We all feel so busy and driven by so many things that make it tough to even catch your breath. I think it is important that we reacquaint ourselves with old ideas like extended conversations and sharing meals and forget the notion that complex problems are solved by people running around with their 'heads cut off.'

Aaron: Norman, you've talked about the opportunities you had in university to reflect with some great thinkers and social activists...

Norman: When I went to York University I got myself into regular classes at the regular school, even though what they wanted to do was put me into the segregated class in the regular school. For me, being in a regular class was just a matter of problem solving. After I graduated high school, I went to York University. A person who lived in residence invited me to speak in Marsha Forest's class. She was really enthused about the idea of inclusion and we started working together. And because I was at York, I also got to know Judith Snow, who was, at that time the director of the Centre for Disabled Students at York. She was working as a liaison with one of my professors. Marsha was very excited about having me talk about my experiences as a student with a disability in a regular classroom, and she said, "we need to take these ideas to the conferences". You know, at the time I was more interested in beer and pinball and trying to sleep with girls. So, I said, "Nah." But, I told Marsha that the person who could really help is Judith. So, I am the person who introduced Judith to Marsha. And we know the history there! The National Institute (G. Allan Roehr Centre) pulled me in and invited me to all their training. That's where I got to hear people like John O'Brien and others. All that training was done less than 100 yards from my residence, so it was easy to get over there and spend the weekend with people like John O'Brien and Herb Lovett. It was such a luxury.

The overwhelming thing I found was that all the stuff that I had learned as a person with a physical disability also applied to people with mental disabilities. That blew my mind. I had always thought that they were completely separate issues.

Another pivotal point for me was a summer institute at McGill University when I participated in a two week intensive course with John McKnight. That just took it to a new level, because that's when he started talking about the idea that the problem was not with people, but more with the social structure we use. He approached it from a sociological point of view. I had never heard this analysis before. I realized that we were using the wrong tools. For example, we were using a bureaucratic structure that was specifically designed to get rid of deviation. It was specifically set up so that if one person doing a job got removed, another person could just come in and take over. We were designing a bureaucracy to run trains on time, to do mass production of items, etcetera. We thought that because this works so well with the production of things, let's use it on people! If we just got the right people, we thought, we could make it work.

But, understanding it from a sociological perspective, it's like trying to bake a cake in a washing machine. A washing machine is great for washing clothes, but you can't bake a cake in it. But we don't get that. We keep trying to change the recipe, hoping that if we just get the recipe right we'll get a lemon meringue pie at the end of the spin cycle.

And that was the real awakening for me. That prompted me to read in related fields that were not necessarily being read by people in our field. I was reading John O'Brien's stuff, of course, and Judith's, but I got more interested in the British disability stuff. Guys like Mike Oliver, for example, who comes from a place of historical materialism, basically a neo-Marxist perspective. This all tied in to John McKnight's idea that in North America we assume that people have disabilities as a matter of chance – you're just born that way – so let's do something to make sure you're supported and have a good quality of life. Mike Oliver believes that disability is actually an inevitable consequence of capitalism. As long as we have capitalism and individualism, we will necessarily disable people who have noticeable impairments.

So that just piled upon John McKnight's stuff, and my view kept getting bigger and bigger, and now I'm involved in writing this book that I'm really excited about. It's a humanistic perspective around how we build more person-centred services by explaining this first from a perspective that draws in economic structure and how that disables people, but also looking at current thinking in disability studies. People like Tom Shakespeare, Miriam Corker and Shelley Tremain, who are looking at all this from a post-structural point of view. We (Emma and I) are trying to take all this mainly academic stuff and make it a) accessible and b) practical. Because it's great learning from Foucault, who really describes the problem of disability beautifully. Unfortunately, though, the writing is quite arcane and academic, making it difficult for many people to engage with. And in addition, while Foucault eloquently makes the connection between professional knowledge and professional power, and how that oppresses people, he doesn't help us think about what we need to do about that now. He never quite gets there. So, right now, Emma and I are having a great time thinking about how to take that stuff and apply it to a more pragmatic idea.

Paul Young

interviewed by Patrick McDonagh

Patrick: Tell me how you got involved with People First[1].

Paul: I was involved with the cross-disability local chapter in Sydney, Nova Scotia, and had been involved about nine years, and that's where I learned about the issues around disability. One day, I was listening to a local phone-in show, and I heard a man by the name of John Cox talking about People First. I had heard at another conference, at the cross-disability provincial conference, about a man talking about People First, but had no more information about it. Then when I heard Mr. Cox on the radio, it sounded like something I should get involved in because I had been labelled handicapped and I had been in a sheltered workshop and in segregated schools before that. So I made a phone call to him and we met at a local hotel in Sydney and shared some thoughts and concerns. We started to develop People First of Nova Scotia. At the same time I heard of a national project committee trying to start People First groups across the country. I asked to get involved with that, and then sat on the founding executive of People First of Canada as the first vice-chair. Then, three years after, I became the president of People First of Canada. That's how I got involved, that's why I'm involved, or one of the reasons. One of the reasons it's important to me is because of the early life history I have had. I was very lucky to get out of what I call the cocoon of impossibility, meaning sheltered, segregated classes, workshops, the traditional services that people with intellectual disabilities receive.

I thought that now that I have the so-called good life, other people with my history should have the same opportunities. In a very quick capsule, I can tell you that, as I said, I was in a segregated classroom, and in a sheltered workshop. I spent 12 years there and met some people who were instrumental in teaching me and helping me to get into radio. I spent 18 years as an audio technician at *CBC* in Sydney, Nova Scotia. So I made big money, I've gone on a lot of trips, vacations to Florida, I even bought and paid for a house, learned how to drive a car, bought a

---

[1] People First of Canada / Personnes D'abord du Canada is a social justice movement founded in the early 1970s by people who had been labelled and, often, had lived in institutions. Every province and territory of Canada, and many of the United States, as well as other countries, has People First groups which are run by elected boards, supported by "advisors." See www.peoplefirstofcanada.ca for more information.

car, all these things.

I've climbed up the mountain to where the freedom is: freedom of choice, freedom of association, freedom to be secure and, as I said, to make your own choices.

But not all the people with my experiences have had the same chances and opportunities that I have had.

Patrick: How do you break out of that cocoon of impossibility?

Paul: I was very lucky to have met the right people at the right time. I think that we need to put supports in place, for all life aspects: put supports in place for education, put supports in place for living in your own community, put supports in place for having your own place whatever aspect of life, there needs to be support around that so a person with a label - whatever the label is at that time - will be given the opportunity to have choices.

The day I met Stewart Marsh, a doctor who owned a private radio station, I asked him if I could hang around there and run errands. He gave me a job at $25 a week so I wouldn't lose my disability pension. Then I met some people who were at *CBC*, including a technician at *CBC*, Walter Pretty, who took me under his wing to teach me how to be an audio technician. He not only taught me how but helped me to become qualified to get a full-time job at *CBC*. That was all voluntary. I think that programs of support need to be set in place so that we can have a good life and have freedom to make our own choices. For people to start doing that with the kind of experiences I have had is getting involved not with self-advocacy, because I think it's different, but with People First, which is an organization of people with the same history, talking about their stories, listening to each other, relating to the experiences or learning from the experiences. That gives us the strength to say as a group, "this is what we want."

Patrick: How is that different from self-advocacy?

Paul: Well, I think that self-advocacy is more around people advocating for themselves. There's nothing wrong with that, but there's always strength in numbers. I think a lot of areas within the movement of People First, or in the outer circle of People First, people have become known as "self advocates." Whether you are disabled or able-bodied, we all advocate for ourselves. The term has become a distinction; instead of using the "r" word or instead of using "developmentally delayed" or "intellectually challenged" or whatever, being a "self-advocate" has become the new label. So [a single self-advocate] is not as effective as a strong consumer driven movement like People First. That's my belief, that's where I stand, that's what I believe in and that's what I fight for every single day of my life.

Patrick: And you are now leading the *Council of Canadians with Disabilities.*

Paul: Just last June (2000) - I should know the date, I believe it was June 11 - I become the *Chair of the Council of Canadians with Disabilities*, which is where I originally started from, the cross-disability consumer movement. It's a national organization of people with disabilities speaking for themselves, "having our own voice" as the slogan says, and telling society that we want the support, we have views, here's what we think. We have been identified as persons with disabilities and we know best what we need. The word "consumer" refers people with disabilities who consume services, whatever the service agency, whether it be *CIB* [Canadian Institute for the Blind], or the *Canadian Paraplegic Association*, or whatever association provides services. People with disabilities consume those services. Before, professionals spoke on our behalf - doctors, professional organizations such as the *March of Dimes* - and those agencies were run by people without disabilities.

Patrick: Do you see this as a rights movement as well?

Paul: Oh, it's definitely a rights movement.

Patrick: I understand the notion of consuming the services, but is it important to articulate that this is fundamentally a human rights concern, that these services have to be provided as a human right?

Paul: Well, it's not just the services but also the opportunity to advance as an individual; for instance, maybe not have to live in some service-oriented place, if someone needs to have their own apartment or house, or whatever. It is more about rights for the person, and rights for the sector that is advocating for these rights. It is very similar to the civil rights movement in the United States. In some ways there are the same issues, and similarities of how to approach the issues. For me its quite exciting because it's not just what I said about wanting other people to have their lives changed and have the opportunities that I've been lucky to have, but to think that people with disabilities are actually speaking out and saying they want their rights. It's a very pioneering thing. Far be it from me to say, but I deeply believe that in a hundred years time the people who are involved in this right now and in the past may be written about or talked about, in how visionary they were. That's my take on it. It's a struggle...

I think you asked me what are the challenges and issues we've faced.

Patrick: Yes, I'm interested in knowing about that - both in specific terms, with specific issues, and generally.

Paul: Well there are a couple of issues, and the obvious issue is to get beyond the stigma of being disabled. And how society has viewed us, is viewing us, it affects the people with my history, it affects people with any disability. People's attitudes have become more of a disability than the disability. The belief that we can't do anything, that we aren't going to be able to contribute to society, that we have nothing to offer, has been brought forth by the charitable models of the agencies and well-meaning people in order to raise money to support or whatever, they have portrayed us in a very bad negative way. Another thing is that the focus is on the disability. They're always trying to fix the "problem," instead of supporting people to get on with their lives, supporting the disability, and finding out who the person is and what makes him or her tick as a person. That, not focussing on the disability, is the key. The "People First" name, the phrase "people first," says it all, because we are people first. The disability is there, yes. Support it. What do I need to be supported with the disability, how can I learn, what do I need to learn, what do I have to offer, what skills did the supreme being or God or whatever you want to call it give me? And that's the important thing, but our society is focused on the disability.

Society, with the global market, values people who make money, people who can present themselves well, look well, and fit the "perfect world"...but there is no perfect world.

The challenges, just to be sure I said it all, are the challenge within the disabled community to become organized, the challenge in the disabled community to get beyond the stigmas and the hurt that society has put on them, and to realize that we need to have our voice heard and to demonstrate to society that we are or should be equal citizens who can contribute to whatever country we are in.

Patrick: You mentioned the global economy and the competitive society - are we looking at something that will require different changes in economic perspective or different ways of valuing people which are not concerned with economics?

Paul: I think the economics is not the problem. It's the attitudes toward people that count. Once the attitude changes, the money will be there. They've been doing deficit reduction in this country and downsizing and putting our value on money, not looking at how do I make a citizen become whatever he or she wants. It's not just by providing them with jobs but providing them with a sense of who they are and what they are about. It may sound not appropriate these days, but people have lost a sense of what it means to be a Canadian. There was before a sense of how could we help those who are not as fortunate as us, and I don't mean in a charitable way, but making sure that the lower end of the scale is not so far from the higher end of the scale. That's been done away with. The poor get poorer and the rich get richer. No-one is taking care of the lower end of the scale and making sure it's not too low; instead, it's the survival of the fittest. That doesn't help people with disabilities.

Patrick: That doesn't help a lot of people - it's interesting because concerns like the one you just raised make this a really broad issue that affects a lot of people, not just those with disabilities. What about the specific issues?

Paul: In People First right now, and in the *CCD*, it's the Latimer case. Other people perceive that people with disabilities are suffering, or that, especially if they are non-verbal, they are no use to anybody. Because of the values that society now has, people are quite frankly in very great danger. No-one should have the right to decide who should die and who should live. I believe that firmly, and I'm very concerned. The Latimer case is going to be very crucial to how we can change society's attitudes toward whether people are accepted or not accepted, and who decides what is suffering.[1]

Patrick: That's a fascinating problem because a lot of people perceive "difference" as a form of suffering.

Paul: Yes, well, if you don't measure up to the well-dressed, well kept, healthy, pretty, beautiful - whatever the phrase - then you must be suffering, you must be different and we don't want difference. And yet society says it wants difference.

Patrick: And it would fall apart without it.

Paul: Well, if we were all the same person, it wouldn't be very good.

Patrick: Thank you, Paul.

---

[1] *Note: in January 2001, Robert Latimer's appeal was rejected by the Supreme Court of Canada, which ruled that he must serve a ten-year sentence for the murder of his disabled daughter Tracy. The verdict remains controversial as many Canadians support Latimer's claim that he was performing a mercy killing and thus should not receive a jail term. P.M.*

The Importance of Belonging

David Pitonyak

"Are there people who are imbued with the belief and hope for a brighter, better future for the person?" Mary Romer

Most of what I do in my practice is not very complicated. I spend time with people in ordinary places and situations and try to get to know them. I always ask the person for permission to meddle in their business, and most people, even those without a formal means of communication, let me know that it's OK. What I am most interested in is the person's story, the people and events that have shaped their lives, the highlights and disappointments, the ordeals and accomplishments. What often emerges, if I listen carefully, is a very human story, one that is easy to identify with, one that is all at once extraordinary and ordinary.

More often than not, what I learn from these stories is that the root of the person's difficult behaviors is loneliness. Many of the people I meet in my practice have one thing in common - they have lost connections to the most important people in their lives. Some people have no contact with their families, or if they do, the contacts are infrequent or tentative at best. Sometimes family members are there, but the person has no friends, depending instead people who are paid to be with them.

Paid care givers can be wonderful company, but they frequently change jobs or assume new positions; the resulting instability can be devastating to someone who is fundamentally alone. Bob Perske (1988) describes how a person whose life is devoid of meaningful relationships might feel: "We have only begun to sense the tragic wounds that so many [persons with developmental disabilities] may feel when it dawns on them that the only people relating with them - outside of relatives - are paid to do so. If you or I came to such a sad realization about ourselves, it would rip at our souls to even talk about it."

I believe that loneliness is the number one cause of difficult behaviors. It is not the only cause, of course, it is just the most common one.

We are relational beings and the absence of meaningful relationships makes us sick. It wears us down to the point where we can't see straight. If you have difficulty believing it, if it seems too "touchy-feely," imagine yourself without the people you love for thirty days. You have no idea where they have gone. Now imagine being without them for sixty days ...or ninety ...or more. How are you feeling? Are you sleeping well? What is your mood? My bet is that you are falling apart. My bet is that you are spiraling out of control. You want to be logical about all of this, but reason has taken a back seat to longing.

I met a man once who was very much alone in the world. When he was a young boy, his family sent him to an institution. He had troubling behaviors, including self-injury, that would not go away, regardless of the behavioral strategies people employed or the medications he was given. He refused to do things with other people and preferred to isolate himself in his bedroom, wrapped tightly in blankets; they said he was "resistant to our treatment efforts." After getting to know him better, I came to believe that his troubling behaviors and his resistance to relationships were the direct result of the trauma he endured when he was separated from his family as a young boy, and from the systematic abuse he suffered at the hands of his "care givers," often in the name of treatment (e.g., time out, seclusion, over-correction). This is to say nothing of the constant turnover in his staff; losing them was common; losing the people he cared about was less common though far more devastating.

When I suggested that trauma and loneliness might be at the root of his difficulties, one member of his team said, "He's not lonely. He has one-to-one coverage." You can, of course, have ten-to-one coverage and be terribly alone. One way I like to explain the difference between coverage and relationships is to ask people to imagine that I have just returned home from a road trip. I pull up in my driveway, and discover that my wife, Cyndi, is not home. Another woman is standing at the door and I ask, "Where is Cyndi?" She replies, "Cyndi is not home, but don't worry. We have you covered."

People generally laugh at this scenario; it's silly; preposterous, really. But it is exactly what happens to people who experience our services time and time again. The very fact that people laugh at the joke of another woman "covering" for my wife is indication that they know there is a huge difference between "coverage" and "relationships." Our field keeps giving people coverage (and interventions) when what they desperately need is to belong.

There are many things we can do to help people find meaningful and enduring relationships (Pitonyak, 2004). As a starting point, I like the questions posed by Mary Romer (Romer, 2002). They strike me as fundamental to anyone's success: "Are enough people engaged in the person's life?" "Are there people who are imbued with the belief and hope for a brighter, better future for the person?" and, "If not, how might such people be found or how might that sense of hope be instilled in those committed to walking with the person?"

Powell River Conversation
Part Two:
"Rafts, Boats and Anchors"
Julia Downs, Maria Glaze,
Aaron Johannes, Norman Kunc,
David Pitonyak, Shelley Nessman,
Jim Reynolds, Susan Stanfield,
Alison Taplay, Emma Van der Klift

Emma: There are a few really pivotal experiences I had early in my exposure to this field. The first thing I ever did in my job, in 1975, was attend a Marc Gold seminar. It was radically life-changing. Marc Gold said if you're trying to do things and they don't work, don't keep doing them in the same way; try another way. At the time, I worked in a group home, which at that time was considered state-of-the-art. It was developed by parents at the request of their daughter, a young woman with a developmental disability. When her siblings were leaving home, she asked her parents "How come I can't live on my own?" And they thought, yes, why not? So, a group of parents got together and opened a group home for *ten* people. The staff and residents were all the same age, which created some interesting dynamics. Actually, we had a wonderful time. We did all sorts of things that we weren't supposed to do. We went to the bar with people. We had water fights in the kitchen. We were all teenagers and young adults. I still remain in contact with some of those people to this day. None of them, I believe, live in any kind of group home settings any more. They have all gone on to other things. A question that I've asked myself is what allowed that transformation from a pretty custodial service model to a more self directed way of living? What I know now is that it wasn't that those ten people changed and somehow became more able, it was all about our perception of them. We changed.

Another pivotal experience at that time was visiting the institutions. I think one of the first in-services that one of our directors sent us off on was to visit Glendale. We visited just a week after there had been a fatal accident on Shawnigan Lake. A number of people had drowned. A raft had overturned and they were in their wheelchairs, strapped down. We were invited upstairs to visit with the institution doctor in his lab. This was, by itself, a most peculiar experience, visiting an autopsy room in a place that staff vehemently insisted was "home" to its residents. The doctor said, "Come and look at what I have under my microscope." He showed us a brain slide of one of those individuals, and said, "Look. You can see here where the white matter is protruding into the grey matter, and that is probably the genesis of the mental disability." At that moment, I was radicalized in some important way. Something happened to me there. It engendered an outrage and made me excruciatingly aware of the many, many ways in which people are robbed of their dignity and humanity.

Another pivotal experience was that during the time we spent helping people to move out of institutions back into community, fully five of the people that we brought home were siblings of people that I had gone to school with. I never even knew they existed! That was just mind-boggling – a huge revelation. As Alison mentioned, we were involved with creating some more person-centred situations as we went along – some that persist to this day and are really quite wonderful. But predictably, the bricks and mortar persist as well, as they do when we build and buy those things. Together with government agencies, we colluded to do that stuff. I mean, that was the thinking of the day. We were invited to "get the financial resources into your community (through the development of group residences) and then you can decide what to do with the money more creatively later"...well, we know that this didn't happen often for most organizations.

I am a strong believer in cross-pollination between fields. I think we become stagnant when we continue to look at the same issues through the same lenses. We need to engage in dialogue in unexpected places in order to engender unexpected insights, I think. For example, some of the recent work that I have done is with hostage negotiators, with a view to gaining alternative perspectives about what gets euphemistically called "challenging behavior". I wanted to talk with them about the relational strategies that they use in helping people who are the most distressed of just about anybody on the planet – at a time when they are at their most distressed and quite dangerous – to deescalate. These people usually have weapons and are threatening to kill themselves or others. It turns out that de-escalation is accomplished with words, not weapons. And it is very much relational. It is done by changing their mind-set about who that person is and why they're doing what they're doing.

Rather than seeing this person as a deranged and dysfunctional criminal who's got a gun, they told me that what they see is "just a person in a bad place". They can't be judgmental or authoritarian. They say that if you don't change your view of the person, your judgment leaks in. And then anything you try to do will re-escalate the person. The stakes are really high! If you blow it, people die. Despite what you see on TV, hostage negotiators are successful in more than 90% of the negotiations that they conduct. The people I talked with – the guy that did the Lufthansa negotiations, for example – said they are successful almost all the time. 90% is a conservative estimate. It is more like 95%, and it is all done with words. Forget about the SWAT team and the Kevlar vest; that is almost all for TV. I guess what I'm saying is that I think it is important that we look at what other people in other places are doing, and not just fall into the trap of sticking with the same old formulas and ideas. The old formulas are simple, they're easy. But, surprisingly, so is the other stuff. The negotiators told me, this is not rocket science, this is relational – and it works.

Alison: Part of my desire is to support parents and others who are providing paid or unpaid support to people who experience disabilities is to assist them to become more reflective about what they are doing, to develop reflection as a habit; in other words to be habitually curious and reflective.

Aaron: And that idea is something that the creation of this conversation over the course of a whole day has brought up for all of us – the rarity of opportunity for reflection and chances to discuss and rethink ...even for us. And how much more rare is it for staff and support workers at the ground level, or government organizations where they've made this insane choice to change a system while concurrently cutting funding. In such environments, how do we learn and grow?

Julia: The Family Support Institute is where I came into contact with Norman and got involved organizing Family Focus conferences and networking with people and organizations. To me one of the most important things we do is networking, whether it is with families, or professionals, or people involved in the community. And like David [Pitonyak] said yesterday in a presentation I attended, "The universe always provides when you're ready." That talk made me think about what we're doing and to look at some things we're doing and how we can make positive changes. Today's discussion, for me, is really perfect timing.

Aaron: I feel like I need to tell this story. In my family, I really liked reading and art but everyone else farmed and hunted and worked, but this one favourite uncle read history books and wanted to talk about them just as much as I wanted to talk about books. He knew all kinds of thing about this bigger world and loved to discuss politics.

So, I grew up, a bunch of things happened, and then I ended up in this field quite accidently really, and I was talking to a group of recreation therapy students one day, showing them pictures of folks with disabilities engaged in recreation and talking about how everybody needs recreation. I looked at this one picture and I suddenly went, "Oh my God! Uncle Jerry has a disability." I mean, he had a cane, and sometimes a walker, and he had a lot of trouble holding on to things, and all these things came together, like how when we went out and he talked to people they'd look at me to translate what he was saying.

So, I phoned my Mom and said, "Uncle Jerry has a disability!" And she said, "Why would you say a thing like that!?" She was ready to punch someone out. She said, "Well he's not disabled like people with disabilities are disabled." And ever since, I have come to think this is what all of us who know and care about people with disabilities come to think and feel. They are no longer "them," they are "us." In an interview Chester Finn is talking about developing community and he says this great thing, that once people get to know us, they can't hardly help but want to help us. And in many of the oral histories and interviews with self advocates they talk about this idea that when they've made friends of people, those people become allies in a whole new way.

I used to spend summers with my grandparents, and one day I was waiting for Uncle Jerry to come home. I was walking around the yard, hunching one shoulder up, twisting one hand, and dragging one leg behind me, I was imitating the coolest person in my world that I knew. And my Grandfather, the most gentle man, screeched up in his car, leapt out and slapped me and said, "Don't ever do that again." He was so angry he was trembling. I had never seen him angry before.

For years when I thought about this I thought, wow, he must really have been having a really bad day. But, all of a sudden, all of this stuff came together. My Mom began by saying, "He doesn't really have a disability," but as the years went on told me other things. She said that my grandparents would routinely get invitations to events that didn't include him, and my grandmother just decided to write his name under theirs and send back the RSVP, year after year. The realization that Uncle Jerry had a disability was an initial move for me from "doing" to reflecting on what we were doing. And I got to see, in effect, when I looked back on his life, someone in a downward spiral that had to do with services, who ended up in increasingly specialized group environments where he would have outbursts and then accrued more and more labels.

What he wanted, and had a various brief intervals but *never* because of services, was a job, a wage, independence, a place to call home, a girlfriend and people who cared about him. Here was a guy who had so much capacity and yet just went down and down and down because people like myself were not listening to what he wanted, but insisting that he fit himself into one of our really great three choices or six choices or nine...

Shelley Nessman once said to me, "Everything important in my life, everything I have learned that has helped me to grow, to be who I am, who I really like, has had to do with people with disabilities." It kind of moved my foundations. Because I think as we know and care and love people with disabilities we end up radicalized – there is no choice as we see how they are dealt with by medical, educational and governmental systems that continually try to slot them into little holes. We are constantly aware of the unfairness and built in limitations of these automatic responses.

Susan: In terms of context, a couple of the other pieces that we're anchored our work in is getting away from acronyms and technical language and taking big ideas and explaining them to the people who implement those things in ways that are not formulaic – a little knowledge can be a dangerous thing – it's almost better that people not know how to do PATHs if they're going to do them out of the wrong context or in the wrong way.

We need to explain things in plain language and show them that there are many ways of doing something, individualized ways. The idea of a PATH is not to go through the steps and get the product, the document. It's about who's there and it's one way and not something that works for everyone. Another part of the context so agencies are not adopting just another formula, not say they don't do ISPs anymore but PCPs now – person centred planning now – like it's the same thing. But also how do we get out of this loop of reinventing the wheel. And doing things within the same structure in the same way, baking a pie instead of a cake because we couldn't bake a cake so lets bake a pie in this washing machine even though what people really wanted was a cake and we needed an oven...

Our agency just went through a big strategic planning process a couple of years ago – solicited input from everybody – and we're talking about successorship – no one wants to think about it... no one wants to know about it...

But we are doing these two things – looking at our strategic plan and thinking about successorship – and wondering instead of trying to replace ourselves, building the leadership to continue the organization, what would happen if we hand over power to the people who use our services? David and Michael Kendrick and others we've worked with say don't be so eager to say there won't be a need because there might still be a need for agency support. But in our vision for the future it's not about constantly tweaking the agency to be more person-centred, because it's that thing you talk about Norm – that we're in a structure that is inherently at odds with the idea that people can control their own lives. So how do you shift the balance of power – this issue of agencies holding so much control over people's lives is the central issue.

Alison: In a big way it's about real estate – so many agencies got real estate by developing services while paradoxically people who have disabilities remained real estate poor.

Susan: Yes, shackled to real estate – we have three one million dollar homes – and lots of agencies have way more than that. This other organization did all this fund raising a decade ago and built this amazing building – I have no idea how much it's worth – and it's the most beautiful facility, the nicest day program you've ever seen. People come from all over town to it. They don't want to leave they don't want to change things – they're so dedicated to this – the board did all this funding-raising and it was so successful. And they are not alone, there are places like that all around the country.

David: I like to refer to that as the 'addiction to the boat.' Imagine there's a lake in front of you and there's a boat on the shore and your goal is to get across the lake. As a strategy, the boat makes a lot of sense. So you get in the boat and you go across the lake.

The problem with our profession is that we get addicted to the boat. When we land on the other side of whatever it is, we still think we need the boat and, with much determination, carry it overland. We get addicted to the process – functional assessments, person-centered-plans, risk assessment, whatever it might be - and we don't realize that we've gotten to the other side and now its about our relationships.

Alison, this thing about being in a private place that is shared with a few and maybe there are some things about yourself that are just yours, I don't think the boat can make it happen. It is so dependent on the quality of our relationships. They may deepen because the boat was helpful along the way, but it's about a lot more than the boat.

Maria: Our youngest daughter, Kate, came into our lives when I was feeling quite cocky as a Mom. I had been super vigilant in my interactions with Rebecca, making sure I followed every recommendation every professional ever made. I was still in the early intervention mind set. I was praised by professionals for my "work" with Rebecca and was feeling very sure of myself.

Kate initially came into our lives at 18 months of age as one of the children attending my family day care, later as our foster child, and then as our own daughter through adoption. By the time we adopted Kate she had collected an assortment of "labels" herself. Gifted was one of them. Kate was incredibly strong willed, pushed lots of my buttons and came into my life with many teaching opportunities at a time I needed them. I had an "ah ha" moment one night at the dinner table when I was having a meal with both my daughters. The way I was supporting Rebecca through each meal-time was setting every moment up as a learning opportunity. For example, I would pour her a very small amount of juice and give her very small amounts of food. I would support Rebecca to use the spoon with hand over hand assistance. When she finished each tiny portion she would have to "earn" more food and drink by using a sign language approximation, or by making a sound indicating "more, eat or juice."

I looked at Kate and thought, here is my youngest daughter, labeled as gifted, and I'm not holding up flash cards saying, "You want more potatoes? Spell potato, now spell it backwards, now say it in French." Kate would never have tolerated this and I probably would have ended up wearing the potatoes, but we were teaching Rebecca "compliance." I thought of Norman and his story of stairs going nowhere and the Credo for Support ("do not try to fix me because I am not broken" were words that haunted me ever since I first read them). I look at what I created for her to get a meal because of her label of developmental disability and realized what a double standard I had for my two daughters. It didn't seem fair. Norman was the first person who talked to me about what it felt like to be the person being "worked on," and how it might feel to be seen as "deficient." It was very hard to hear and to see myself through those eyes. Hearing Norman created a huge shift in the lens I looked through when I saw Rebecca and my role in her life. So at the dinner table, with Kate's help, I was able to think about what it might feel like to be Rebecca and have a Mom who never let up trying to teach her. That was what I was trying to illustrate with my story of that dinner.

You know, had I not heard Norman, I'm not sure I would have been ready to see things from that perspective. Prior to hearing Norman speak so many years ago, I had attended some conferences and workshops mostly with professionals presenting on intervention techniques, or hearing other parents talk about their experiences. My life (and Rebecca's) had become about identifying goals – things to be "worked on" - and then working on them. I think at times I forgot about the child behind the "measurable goals." Yes, this shift in my thinking was informed, in a large part, by hearing Norman talk about what that kind of treatment is like for people. I love his notion of the special education SWAT team. I was the early intervention SWAT team, and I was going to program that disability right out of my kid.

And autism is seductive that way. You are lead to believe that you can do it. You feel like a failure if you don't do everything that professional people tell you will help. One more thing I will say about this: the early intervention program in Calgary had a time out room. It was a padded, windowless room. There was one time I was there doing the program with my daughter. I was there because I wouldn't send my 2 year old for four days a week without me, as was recommended. No, if my daughter was going to learn something, I was going to learn it too. I had to clear out of the way with my daughter one day, because somebody was being dragged kicking and screaming into the time out room. Somebody had gotten a bloody nose from this person, so they threw him in the time out room, and for half an hour we saw the plaster crack and we could hear him kicking to get out. And, at that time, I was struggling with this program I was doing with my daughter, because there were times when she would cry so hard that her nose bled.

They told me that the poor guy in the time out room was there because he didn't have the benefit of an early intervention program. They said to me, "You don't want to end up like that, do you?" I was terrified that if I didn't keep doing this that the time out room would become my daughter's future – our future. They were so harsh with that poor guy, and I didn't want that for us. So I was like, "Okay Becky, feet down, hands down, look at me." And we would get started. I didn't want us to end up like that guy in the time out room. And that was my introduction to supporting someone. And Norman, you came in with your "Credo for Support" and talked to us and challenged all of that. It was hard, but it made me really think about what I was doing, and I thank you for that; and Becky thanks you for that.

Norman: Thank you for that, Maria. When we do this stuff, we usually show up, we present, and then we go away. We rarely get to hear feedback. Of course, I can't take sole credit for "The Credo of Support" – Emma and I wrote it together.

Aaron: "The Credo of Support" has been, for a lot of people in North America, certainly in Canada, one of the most important documents in terms of moving people to a different way of thinking about their lives and in terms of getting self advocates and their supporters to think differently about their lives.

Rekindling Commitment:
reflections from a pastoral educator enmeshed in direct support professional workforce development and person centered supports

W. C. Gaventa

Relying on compliance

It was 20 years ago at an American Association on Mental Retardation (AAMR) Conference in Los Angeles. I was talking to Francis MacIntosh, a former chaplain at a developmental centre in California, who had moved into a new role in the Quality Assurance Department. These were the heydays of active treatment, long and very specific interdisciplinary developmental plans for individuals for their programmes and staff, growing numbers of regulations and standards that sought to protect the health and safety of individuals with intellectual disabilities (ID) being served on the one hand and, on the other, to protect the systems from the kinds of abuse and neglect (and subsequent bad publicity) that still happened too frequently in either institutional or community-based services. Mac, as he was called, made a statement that I have never forgotten: "In a system that does not know how to enhance commitment, it relies instead on compliance."

The intent of this reflection and commentary is to explore that dilemma. What are the pressures in the systems of care that push towards compliance? Is the result what Ivan Illich called "paradoxical counter-productivity", i.e. a system trying to help people be safer actually becomes less so (Schwartz 1996)? Taylor (1992), as part of issue of *Mental Retardation* containing the papers on a symposium on compliance and quality in residential life, defined the paradox of compliance with regulations in the following way:

> Herein lies the paradox: In order to meet the regulations, a setting or a home must become more impersonal, hierarchical, and bureaucratic, and these are some of the features that made institutions dehumanizing and abusive in the first place.

How can the commitment and compliance be rebalanced? How can commitment be enhanced?

If anything, that dichotomy and paradox have grown over the past 20 years. Our systems of services and supports call for professionals and direct care staff to have a broader array of skills and a deeper commitment to the vision and ideals of the systems in which we work (Larson & Hewitt 2005; U.S. Department of Health and Human Services *et al.* 2006). Professionals are not only to assess and treat from their chosen professional disciplines but also to provide direct care in ways that fulfil the dreams and goals in an individual habilitation plan. They are to provide specific kinds of daily living skills and care, teach skill development, empower "consumer participation and choice," help connect and include people in inclusive community settings, and serve as effective advocates for the families and systems with whom they work. In the United States, the value base of independence, productivity, inclusion and self-determination is written into the federal Developmental Disabilities Act (DDACT2). That vision calls for professionals who are knowledgeable, skilled, creative and committed. Quality of life, person-centred care and outcomes, self-directed services and supports are all mantras in the values and visions that drive our systems of care and support (Keeping the Promises 2003; O'Brien J. with staff from Creative Living Services 2004; Larson & Hewitt 2005; U.S. Department of Health and Human Services *et al.* 2006).

But along with those values, visions and skills comes an increasingly complex web of regulations and legal requirements. Our systems import the language of customer service from the business world, yet the real customer which drives the system is often the funding streams from public sources on which they depend. On a large system-wide basis, those funding streams can only attempt to enhance quality by system-wide regulation and policy. (Mulick & Meinhold 1992; Taylor 1992). That can too often feed into attempts at system-wide fixes for individual problems, leading to more complex habilitation plans, more licensing regulations for individual programmes, larger and bigger charts and longer policy manuals with more specific procedures, and, when abuse or accidents continue to happen, increasingly specific laws that criminalise poor professional judgment or behaviour (Polzer 2007; New Jersey Office of the Public Advocate 2007), and, e.g. Danielle's Law in New Jersey (New Jersey Office of the Public Advocate 2007).

Let me share a collage of examples and stories in the last decade from experiences in New Jersey and elsewhere.

•   More than 10 years ago, I led a workshop with a faith network. One congregational representative said his church had developed a relationship with the people who lived in a local group home, doing things beyond just inviting them to church such as working together to plant and nurture a garden. But, as the crops were harvested, they were told that the people could not eat them, because their produce did not fit the dietary plans and food procurement/preparation processes in the agency that ran the home.

•   A professional in New Jersey who had done some pioneering work in paying attention to the sexual needs and interests of adults with developmental disabilities went on to develop a training and procedure manual for direct care staff, and to market both the manual and her role as trainer. That was admirable, but she continued on to say that the manual comprehensively covered all the policies and procedures any agency would need, so that, once trained, "direct care staff would not even have to think" when faced with a situation involving sexuality. Professional direct care, once again, was reduced to following the plans, procedures or regulations as outlined by others.

•   In New Jersey, with an increase in projects that focused on learning the skills of community building, it became more apparent that we were asking direct care staff to help individuals participate in communities that were foreign to the staff as well as to the individuals. They were foreign because staff could not afford to live there and/or they came from other cultures, countries or communities in which community life was much different. If community building depends on building relationships, which it does, then those initiatives were "handicapped" from the beginning.

•   A couple of years ago, the New Jersey state government passed a new law called "Danielle's Law" (New Jersey Office of the Public Advocate 2007), whose impetus came from an avoidable death of a young woman in a group home, leading to a political movement by frustrated parents and friends who wanted the political system to prevent anything like that from happening again. It is not unlike a number of similar laws with names attached to them, which end up trying to correct instances of poor judgment with a series of regulations and procedures that simply call for compliance, with financial and disciplinary consequences if they are not followed.

•   At an international symposium in France funded by the Templeton Foundation, participants heard Jean Vanier, founder of the international L'Arche communities, talk about some of the dilemmas facing their staff and homes. L'Arche is built on the commitment of its staff, volunteers and supporters, but recently has had to enter the licensing and regulatory jungles in order to receive some public funding. He noted that compliance with building codes almost bankrupted them because of physical changes that had to be made to homes in which people had been safely and happily living for years.

Anyone could list their own examples. The paradoxical result is too often service systems and care that are based on fear rather than a positive vision of growth, development and participation. There is the fear of abuse, fear of risk, fear of discipline, fear of bad publicity, fear of making a mistake, fear of failure, all compounded by a fear of loss of funding. Fear does not enhance commitment; it feeds compliance (Holburn 1992; Maister 1997). Accountability is to the regulators, inspectors or the outcomes in an individual's plan, not to the relationship with the people one supports and/or to fellow staff and families. Add to all that the fact that many service agencies are large, top down, bureaucratic organisations, where the ones doing the most direct care are the ones with the lowest pay, the ones expected to follow the input of others without a lot of input or voice into the management systems and plans of care, and the ones often directly supervised by people who have recently been promoted without any training in management or good supervisory skills, then one is playing with a recipe for disaster (Ebenstein 1996; Hatton *et al.* 2001; Hewitt *et al.* 2004). That disaster is being seen in huge turnover of direct care staff in many service organisations throughout the United States, often a vicious cycle in itself where turnover and vacancies lead to frenetic and sometimes frantic (i.e. fearful) attempts to hire enough people to provide basic care, but whose lack of training and longevity create more mistakes, more attempts to control or prevent them by rules, regulation and punishment, then more turnover (Frank & Dawson 2000; Hewitt *et al.* 2004; Larson & Hewitt 2005; U.S. Department of Health and Human Services *et al.* 2006).

The impact is not hard to see or imagine. One example is a story I heard from a workshop presentation on direct support professional supports at the Alliance for Full Participation, a large national conference in the United States in September of 2005, sponsored by 11 national disability networks. An agency in upstate New York, known for its leadership in supporting and training its staff, had taken one of its "consumers" in her late 50s and researched, from the records, the number of staff who had been caregivers in her life, from the present going backwards. They stopped counting at 500 (Demar 2005).

As we worked on the rationale for a state-wide career path pilot grant in New Jersey the next year, one quote by an Associate Director illustrated the same impact:

> Turnover and vacancies have a significant impact on the quality of lives of the individuals we support. All of the services and supports we provide are anchored in relationships, relationships between the individuals and the people who support them. You cannot effectively support someone unless you know them and they you and they trust you and you them. Direct support professionals are involved in the most intimate aspects of people's lives. They know their hopes and dreams, comfort them through disappointments and tragedy, celebrate the good times, provide reassurance when sick or even dying. How can this be done if the individual does not have a relationship with the staff person? How can a relationship be built when there is a different person every few weeks or months or worse when a position is vacant, a substitute or a different temp every day. If a person does not feel supported, then are we really providing support? (Kathy Walsh, Associate Director, Arc of Bergen County. Survey response)

There are so many factors impacting the rates of turnover and retention for direct care workers in the United States. The factors that often receive the most attention are wages, training, worker benefits, supervision and management (Frank & Dawson 2000; U.S. Department of Health and Human Services *et al.* 2006). The ways in which increasing regulation and control impacts job satisfaction and workforce culture are factors for which most everyone I know can cite anecdotal evidence, but comprehensive studies are difficult to find, with a few exceptions (Shea 1990; Holburn 1992; Mulick & Meinhold 1992; O'Brien & O'Brien 1994; O'Brien *et al.* 2004; Cherry *et al.* 2007). Whether the source for enhanced regulation is concern about health and safety, honouring rights, meeting laws and/or an underlying fear that we cannot rely on the caregivers because of the turnover or lack of skill; we end up building a system based more and more on compliance, on regulations, programme and behavioural plans and competencies, without the same kind of attention to the person who are doing the caring, their motivation and what they need. So how, on the other hand, can we enhance commitment?

Promising developments and attached risks

There are already a number of changes in the system of services and supports in the United States that provide hopeful and promising signs. Other countries may indeed have initiatives that are even more promising, but my perspective is shaped and limited by the system(s) in which I work. There are also associated risks, especially in systems of service that too often try to take promising practices that depend on committed relationships and mandate them on a much wider scale, or try to, as we say, "bring them to scale" while also trying to simplify, standardise and reduce costs in manners that are more characteristic of large systems or corporations.

First, there is in the United States a growing focus on person-centred planning and self-directed services and supports. Person-centred planning and services can happen in traditional agency-based services as well as in new forms of "consumer-driven" services, which means individualised budgets over which a person with a disability and his/her family and guardians have controlled. I recognise that one of the premises of this collection of articles is that consumer driven services and management styles based on them have a number of flaws, but when done well, there is great promise for creating new forms of relationship and commitment. Why? For several reasons:

1   The planning process starts with, and should involve, the people with whom someone already has relationships. Direct care and clinical professionals have key roles, but the assumption is that family, friends and other forms of relationship are key to quality of life and planning. For example, O'Brien & O'Brien (1997) use a framework in which they suggest that a person being served needs at least five kinds of relationships: anchors, allies, assistants, agendas (i.e. planners) and associations;

2   The planning often highlights the need for relationship development, with both staff and, with the help of staff, others in the community. Nurturing and maintaining relationships can become important parts of shared learning and care. That is also becoming the focus of some training resources that come out of leaders in person-centred planning and supports, such as those from Inclusion Press (O'Brien & Mount 2001); and

3   When person-centred planning is combined with self-directed funding, the direct care and clinical staff who are hired to fill defined roles have a clearer sense of accountability to the person with whom they are working and the people in that person's circle. In New Jersey, our anecdotal reports are of an improved sense of staff satisfaction in their job, more direct accountability, less frustration with distant supervision and a greater sense of the difference that they make in the lives of those whom they serve. There are problems, including these:

- Good person-centred planning and support development takes a lot of creativity, skill, time and ...commitment. There is a constant temptation in large systems to make it more "efficient", too often leading to what we call "cookie cutter" person-centred plans, or to curious anomalies like computerised plans with multiple choices and drop-down menus. Some of the pressures for those systems go back to the need to demonstrate effectiveness and compliance to funding sources through data driven, objective, measurable outcomes, proving that regulations have been met and standardised units of service delivered.

- The creativity, skill, time and responsibility required also assumes that there are people close to the person with an ID who have the capacity to do so, the ability to manage systems, perhaps to manage and supervise their own staff, and deal with complex funding processes. That may presume a level of education and resources that may not be possessed by a person's family and friends. Empowering people through self-directed services does not necessarily make them good managers or bosses. They may need those skills and that training, just as many front-line supervisors in more traditional service places such as group homes and day programmes (Hewitt & Lakin 2001).

Thus, using person-centred planning process and funding mechanisms that empower people with ID and their families can be a powerful, positive tool. But it also calls for empowering the direct care staff that provide services and supports, or stated in another way and building new forms of partnerships between direct care workers and the people they support (Ebenstein 1996; Hewitt & Lakin 2001).

The second promising trend is the increased focus on workforce development for direct support professionals in the United States. Federal projects, through the Centers for Medicare and Medicaid Services, grass roots initiatives like the National Alliance for Direct Support Professionals, regional and state initiatives by creative provider organisations and state networks and national training initiatives like the online College of Direct Support, are all attempts to help stem the vicious cycles of recruitment, turnover and vacancies with new forms of training, supported by creative management, increased benefits, empowered staff and career paths that allow a good, committed, direct care professional to remain in a direct caregiving role for a longer period of time. As a result of the trend towards person-centeredness and the focus on workforce development, creative managers are recognising a new embodiment of the Golden Rule, i.e. if we are asking direct care staff and others to treat others in person-centred, skilful, committed relationships, then agencies need to treat their staff in the same way.

Focusing on commitment as well as compliance

Given the reliance on public funding for services and supports, compliance with regulations and markers of quality care and assurance are not going away. Evaluation through objective tools and compliance with objective measures are an important part of any system of caregiving and relationships. But how do we pay direct attention to the importance of commitment, and provide the resources and educational opportunities that bring the classic polarities of law and spirit back into a little more balance, i.e. the balance between meeting the letter of law or the spirit of the law, or, in theological terms, focusing on rules and commandments at the expense of "doing justice, loving mercy, and walking humbly" (Micah 6:8).

This need was stated even more succinctly, in a recent television interview on Public Broadcasting Service in the United States between Dr. Bill Thomas (a leader in the development of Green Houses, smaller residential settings for people who are elderly and frail with a focus on patient-centred care, relationships and community) and Susan Dentzer, the correspondent:

> Joyce Ebmeier (Green House Administrator): Death gets harder in a Green House because, when you are smaller and when you are engaged in the way that the shahbazim (their name for quality direct care staff) are engaged in the lives of the elders they love so much, it is like losing your dearest family member.

> Susan Dentzer: All this reminded us of something else Thomas had said back in 2001 about the central problem with nursing homes.

> Dr Bill Thomas: In long term care, love matters. And the heart of the problem is institutions can't love.

> Susan Dentzer: Do you think you've finally helped create a place that can love.

> Dr. Bill Thomas: Yes. In fact, I think it's the signal achievement of the Green House: making a place where love matters (PBS).

How do we create places where love matters? To be incredibly simplistic, we don't control it, but we can create the kinds of necessary and sufficient conditions and structures where it can be fostered, nurtured and encouraged. Most of our services focus on where services happen, what people do to and for others, how it should be done (via the plan), and how often, or when (e.g. Community Supports Skills Standards). What gets disregarded is the "who" of the caregiver and the "why" that person is doing what he or she is doing in the first place, what they learn from it, and hence, the nature of the relationship and commitment between staff and "consumer"[1].

It is true that many organisations and service agencies move towards doing this when they train and reflect on the mission and values of their organisation and its services. Many creative ways of doing that come out of newer forms of understanding management and organisation, such as customer service, the importance of vision and purpose, and structure that allow for creativity and imagination. Flattening the organisation, empowering the front lines, soliciting input, focusing on creative recruitment, training and retention are all markers in this, but one might assume that the importing of business models is still done with the eye towards the consumer and the bottom line (in this case, still too often the regulatory and funding agencies).

What is still missing is a focus on who we are as professional caregivers, our sense of calling and vocation and that which develops and sustains us in caregiving roles that beg for long-term commitment as well as skilled care, i.e. for love as well as good outcomes. To then take "professional" and "caregiving" education further, it is education that focuses on character, community and community. It is education, i.e. a formation of identity and calling, not just on the acquisition of knowledge, skills and techniques.

One of the modern pioneers in this kind of training and professional formation is Parker Palmer, whose work on

---

[1] My biggest problem with the word "consumer" assumes one consumes, and never gives, a label that feeds right into a public stereotype that disability is a black hole into which public investment gets poured while reaping few outcomes or rewards. W.C.G.

community and education led him into projects that initially focused on the formation on the professional development and ongoing commitment of teachers to their vocation. The *Courage to Teach* project focused on education that enabled reflection, honesty, sharing from the heart, openness to a sense of call and vocation and the willingness to act on what is learned. Training opportunities are built, which focus on identity rather than skills, working from the inside out rather than the outside in and a remembering of the powerful role of the teacher, his or her integrity and relationship with the students (Palmer 1997).

What gets in the way of our doing more of this? Palmer (1997) noted the pervasive and primary barrier of fear, a fear not unlike we find in a system of care focused on compliance. He notes three dimensions of fear:

1 Fear in our way of knowing. Valuing objective knowing is, in his perspective, at one level a fear of relationship, a fear of being challenged and changed by what we know and a focus on power over things;

2 Fear in our students, who are often people on the margins (certainly the case in direct care workers), whose fear is not making it, the fear not being valued or being denied; and

3 Fear in our teachers, the fear that we cannot impart to others the knowledge we have, or the commitment we feel.

That work with teachers has led into work on professional formation in other disciplines, including a major initiative with medical education and in particular medical residencies. In a recent article in Change Magazine, from the Carnegie Foundation for the Advancement of Teaching, Palmer (2007) defines the "new professional" as "a person who is not only competent in his or her own discipline but has the skill and the will to deal with the institutional pathologies that threaten the profession's highest standards ...We need professionals who are "in but not of" their institutions, whose allegiance to the core values of their fields makes them resist the institutional diminishment of those values".

Let me suggest that there at least two strategies for rebalancing the equation, all of which are happening in some small but significant ways, but all of which involve fundamental reframing, or expansion, of what is seen to be true, right and important.

The why of commitment: rediscovering the language

One of the opportunities professional caregivers of all levels of skill and responsibility need is the opportunity to reflect on why they do and what they do. Wolf Wolfensberger (1977) noted long ago the phenomenon that one of the prophetic voices and roles of people with ID, to use the terms of the day, was that they were providing a sense of vocation and calling for many, many others. Staff may get asked when they apply for a job why they are interested, but it too often stops there.

There are at least two major reasons why it does not happen more often: finding the language and finding the time, or stated otherwise, building in the opportunity.

Finding the language of relationships and commitment is not a question of there being no language, but there is not a language that has been welcomed, recognised or utilised in any extensive way within modalities of care based either on scientific or on manager/customer frameworks of care. The language of science is the language of objective measurement and proof. John Swinton (2001) has noted that in that in the "world" of scientific caregiving, the "good" becomes that which is observable, the "true" that which is measurable and the "beautiful" that which is replicable. Hans Reinders (2000) explored that world from the perspective of liberal philosophy by noting that in a liberal framework of reason, choice, freedom and rights, the "dignity" of people with ID would always be second class (even with the assumption of equal rights) because of assumptions about their ability to reason and to choose. The corresponding and second major paradox was that a system of care based on those philosophic principles would not be able to understand the reasons that motivated many people to care for, live with and relate to (i.e. be committed to) people with limited intellectual ability.

Finding the language in a system based on liberal public philosophy and scientific principles then means finding a way to reintegrate the languages of relationships: poetry, spirituality, emotions, symbols, art, stories and song. Those are the ways that people talk about their relationships, share the depths of their experiences and find meaning in the depths of what they discover. Thankfully, there are growing examples and indications of this reintegration in many forms: literature and self-story by people with disabilities, poetry, art in amazing forms, recognition of spirituality, theological exploration, cartoons, slogans, symbols and songs. Examples include *Make a Difference: A Guidebook for Person-Centered Direct Support* (O'Brien & Mount 2001) and *"OpenYour Eyes"*, a newly popular rap song written by Sean Delaney, a direct care worker for a direct care worker political rally in Washington. (http://sdotdiz@verizon.net).

One of the most powerful examples for me was a poem written by a direct care worker, Nick Hadju, at an Interfaith Summit related to disability services, reflecting on his relationship with his friend Charlie (a young man, non verbal, wheelchair user):

My Friend Charlie

He is my friend: I am his friend
I help him out: He helps me to learn
I help him to learn: He helps me to grow
I help him to grow: He teaches me to accept

His struggle: Is my struggle
His vulnerability: Leads to my respect
My respect: Leads him to trust
His trust: Leads to my devotion

His availability: Feeds my desire to be needed
I keep his secrets: He keeps mine
        We have an arrangement
His lack of self-consciousness: Leads to my tolerance
His constant need for stimulation: Leads to my patience
His discomfort: Sharpens my sensitivity
His unhappiness: Is my challenge
His presence: Eases my isolation

His loyalty: Leads to my loyalty
     Which leads to mutual appreciation

His brokenness: Makes me accept my own brokenness
     Which leads to healing
His humanity: Leads to personal connection
His steadfastness: Centers me

His smile: Is my reward
His joy: Lifts my spirits
His happiness: Gives me a sense of purpose
His struggles: Expose my anxieties
     Which tests me
     Then strengthens me
     And in turn bolsters my faith

In guiding: I am guided
In helping: I am helped
In teaching: I am taught
In his laughter: There is joy
In that joy: There is energy
In that energy: There is spirit
In that spirit: There is grace

In his eyes: There is a glow
In that glow: Is his soul
In his soul: There is God
And in God: There is peace

(Nate Hajdu Jubilee Association of Maryland, Spoken at the Interfaith Disability PreSummit; September 22, 2005)

Enhancing commitment: making the opportunity

My Friend Charlie is an example of the language of relationship, friendship, mutuality and commitment. At whatever level of caregiving, professionals all have their favourite stories about the people with whom they work and the relationships and experiences that invited and called them into the work they are now doing. What our systems of care so frequently do not have is the opportunity to reflect on those dimensions of caregiving, the invitation to share them with one another and the ways to find, from each other's stories, spirit and depths, a new form of caregiving community which looks, nurtures and draws on the why's of relationship and commitment. Can we hold team meetings, staff retreats and conferences that include times of reflecting on the whys, times for sharing the powerful stories, times for talking about what people within our care do for us while we do for and with them, and times for finding out how others deal with the inevitable periods of dismay, hopelessness and struggle (O'Brien J. with staff from Creative Living Services 2004)?

One of the strategies for doing this also means finding ways and times to talk about and share the spiritual dimensions of professional work and care. Values like independence, productivity, integration and self-determination are at the heart of our systems of care, at least in North America, and at the heart of those values are spiritual questions related to identity (Who am I?) purpose (Why am I?) and community (Whose am I?) (Gaventa 2005). One of the challenges and gifts of working the field of ID is the way that profound philosophical and theological questions are raised, faced and dealt with in living, hands on ways. What are the times, where are the ways, in which we can make the opportunity to share those questions and experiences, learn from them, and together build personal, professional and communal commitment in our relationships with the people we serve and support?

Building in that kind of training and opportunities for reflection and renewal in a system of institutions focused on objective and data driven outcomes and compliance will not be easy. It means reframing the very image of what it means to be "professional", moving away from the expert with the knowledge, power and control, to the professional being called for by people with disabilities and their families, one who walks and journeys with people, assisting through skills but also through mutual relationships of shared responsibility and care (Gaventa 2005). It means recognising that our role is to be value clear, not value free, and that what others need and value from us as professionals is not only technique, programme and procedure, but also a relationship over the long haul in which trust is built, relationships formed and commitments and communities nourished.

Ebenstein (1996), one of the pioneers in work-force development issues in direct care, names the challenge as rediscovering the soul our field, a soul "discovering the complex web and texture of relationships that exist between folks with disabilities and direct service workers", which we do by rediscovering the souls of the workers, the souls of the people we serve and our souls as trainers and managers.

As we do so, perhaps, we will then be able to enhance commitment and rely less on compliance.

Peter Park

interviewed by
Patrick McDonagh

Patrick: How did your association with People First begin?

Peter: I remember in Brantford, people wanted something other than the association, because the association said they would do things, but it might be ten years later ...people wanted something that they owned, they controlled, and so I just used myself as an instrument. I didn't know what I was doing but I started something. That was back in May, 1979.

Patrick: Where does your sense of justice come from?

Peter: I think it's my own personal set of values, maybe it was something that was instilled in me when I was younger. My father was always that way too, and my older brothers. So I grew up in a household where you were conscious of those sort of things - although I wasn't conscious of it.

And I had a cousin who at the time, in the 40s and 50s, was a real pedal pusher. She travelled North America from New York City to Los Angeles at night, was an unescorted woman, would go to Jamaica, was in the Zeigfeild Follies, and was one of the survivors of the Titanic. That right there, I've never thought about it this way before, is where my social values come from.

I keep growing every day, I won't stop learning things. People like Richard [Ruston] for instance, will say "Oh, I'm learning from you, Peter," but I'm learning from Richard. I'm never going to stop learning until I'm put in that hole six feet under. I just feel so positive that things are going to work out for the best.

Patrick: But it's taken a lot of work to make them work out for the best?

Peter: The work in itself is rewarding. It's not just you, it's for us, for everyone. They don't have to live the life that I had. Like being put in an institution for eighteen years, from 20 to 38. If anyone asks my age I'm fifty-nine. But take 18 years off that, and that's my right age, as far as I'm concerned. Because those eighteen years were wasted, and I'm just starting to live. That's the way I look at it, I'm only forty-one.

That's part of history - I know it's important, and I can't forget it. I can't change that. But I don't concentrate on that. I concentrate on what I can change, and I can effect some change for the future, but I can't do anything about the past.

Patrick: You are making sure other people don't use those years.

Peter: That's right. And maybe people wouldn't be at the same stage they're at now otherwise. It's good just seeing other people...

Patrick: You're optimistic for People First and the Rights movement?

Peter: Oh yes. I see this as going along the right way right now. It started with Martin Luther King, who started people thinking more about equality and rights. People First has taken it a step further they're saying it's for people with disabilities too. But we used that for our model.

Patrick: It seems like an exciting movement to be a part of.

Peter: I'm taught by everybody in the movement, and there are people all over Canada. John Cox in Nova Scotia has taught me something. There's people like Arnold Bennington, out in British Columbia, just the opposite end of the country.

Patrick: What are some of People First's triumphs?

Peter: I know that People First was very much involved in the name change, from the *Association for the Mentally Retarded* to the *Association for Community Living*. If it hadn't been for people who had been labelled taking the reins and saying, this is an important issue, it would have been swept under the carpet.

Patrick: What is the most important issue now?

Peter: The Latimer decision now is the most pressing. We don't know when that decision will come down - it went to the Supreme Court, but when they release the verdict, that's a different thing.
   The name change was important, and so was the fact that it helped solidify everybody right across Canada. Maybe we were using different words, but everyone wanted the same thing - we all wanted the name change.

Patrick: It must be challenging to coordinate a group across such a large country.

Peter: Yes, it is very challenging. That's what makes it so rewarding. You'll say "okay, what challenge will I be facing today?" or "I've got to continue working on that challenge." Well, like the name change. People are saying that's over? Well, I'm saying "Hey, what's next?" If you don't keep watch on some of these more powerful people, they're going to say "mentally retarded" again. We don't want that, and we've made it quite clear.

Patrick: How did People First of Canada come about?

Peter: Back in the early 80s, a member from People First of Ontario, went to NIMR to ask them to help him get a grant that would be for something national. At that time it was called the *Self-Advocacy Developmental Project*. There were two people to be hired - the coordinator and a person who had a disability -that was how we wrote it. I happened to be on the hiring committee for the first project. At the time it was called the *Consumer Advisory Committee of CMR* - we hired two people, found that all the time was spent telling people what SADP *self-advocacy developmental project* - was about. It was asked by the funding body if it was alright to change the name to the *National People First Funding Project* rather than something that we had to explain forever and a day, and so finally we got the okay and it was changed. From that we developed a steering committee of members, and the steering committee decided that maybe it was time we became more independent on our own rather than being answerable to the CACL. So they pulled back saying that we wanted a more independent voice, and we couldn't if we were answerable to the board of CAC. So they said, okay, go on your own. So the steering committee made up the first board, and it evolved from there. That was in 1991.

There were provincial associations before the national association. Every province has a provincial association - the only one that doesn't is the new territory, Nunavut.

Patrick: What do you think about the idea of an International People First?

Peter: There's been talk about an international coordinator. Paul

[Young] and I have an idea of where it should go and what it should look like. But other people are afraid, saying "Oh, yes, but then there's funding, there's this other stuff ..." - but let's cross that bridge when we get to it.

I would like to see a coordinated effort by all the international groups, but we have to agree to get together before we can have a coordinated effort. I would like to see something like a federation, a body that's sort of locked in stone, but flexible enough to change somewhere. It would be an International People First, it would be a way of coordinating things with each other. I have visions of how it could work, and I think they would work. Other people have different visions - that's okay too. Paul may have a little different idea from me about what it might look like, so then he and I need to talk about that and we can come to a mutual agreement as to what it should look like. Even at when we're travelling, at conferences at midnight, Paul and I talk - we always make time.

Patrick: What is the role of advisors?

Peter: The role is always changing, depending upon the newness of the group. At first they may be there to take minutes, and they may find themselves helping with other things. They may know more about the court system, from experiences with things like parking tickets, so they're able to give legal advice - their help is based on things that many people haven't experienced.

I think the role is quite unique - it's up to the members to say to the advisor, "Sorry, you're getting too involved. It's time to you to shut up." We make the mistake of not having a working contract with them. I don't know what it would look like, but they should know exactly what is expected of them and when.

Patrick: When did you first get to vote?

Peter: After I got out of institutions. I was still in a group home at that time. If it hadn't been for myself ...they said, "Oh, you've been enumerated with the association," but I found out I had not been enumerated. So I made sure I was. I don't know how I knew that you had to answer all these different questions, but I think that part of it was that I had lived at home, and had seen that happen with my mom and dad and brothers and sisters.

In the institution when I first asked about voting, I was told by a guy, "Peter, you have no rights." I figured that for the 18 years I spent in the institution, because I was such a rebel, I was locked up in *Dewar*, the detention ward, for nine of those years. Mind you, you get locked up for fool things like refusing to take medication that the doctor said, "you are being used like a human guinea pig," so we will refuse to take that medication. That would happen many times with me.

Patrick: Was there a community of people who resisted authorities in the institution?

Peter: There were quite a few people who would say, okay, we'll take the soft side, and few of us who would say, "You guys are all wet." And I was the loudest one to say "You're all wet."

And I made no bones about where I stood. And I don't know how I knew that. But I would say "Hey, I don't agree with you on many things - or most things in fact, not many." People First has taught me a lot about patience and listening. I think that's the biggest thing I've learned. Taking the time to listen. And by listening I mean not just giving an opinion right away, but thinking it through. People don't give that respect to other people. They think, because you are taking that time, "oh well, you're hearing's bad," or something like that. So they shout at you. I don't mean People First members. But it happens.

Patrick: What did you think of the *2000 International Association for the Scientific Study of Intellectual Disability* (IASSID) conference in Seattle? [Peter Park attended this conference at the beginning of August 2000]

Peter: I thought it was very important that we were there, because those are the unconverted people. They don't know a danged thing and their ignorance shows. The whole conference was totally inaccessible escalators, stairs - accessible? Great big words that nobody understood - I don't know if the presenters even understood what they were saying in which case they figure everybody like them is not understanding. So that's fine.

The one person that really annoyed me said "Oh, after talking with you and Paul [Young] I'm including people who have been labelled at all times." He was including them, but not letting them talk. They had a physical presence there. But that's tokenism. He couldn't see it. That led to a big discussion. We pointed this out, and not politely.

I said I will go to the IASSID conference and not the other [on self-Determination and Individualized Funding]. I thought it was more important to go to the conference where I'm talking to the non-converted. Paul Young couldn't get into the conference's opening session because he didn't have a name tag. We were going into the session, and the security person said, "I'm sorry, you cannot go in without a name tag." I said "Pardon me? I would like it to go on record that you can tell the chairperson that I just walked out because if he can't go in, then I won't go." So I didn't go.

I really enjoyed just being able to have the opportunity to bring the issues more to the forefront. I look at it as saying, "That's a challenge to get this on the agenda"

Patrick: Do you think it's on the agenda now?

Peter: I don't think it's that high, but at least its there. And we've got some friends, like Michael Bach, on the inclusion committee, so we've gone a step in the right direction. It may be small right now, but we get more powerful and more powerful as time goes on. People take time to change - it doesn't come in a hurry. At least real change comes slowly. Change that doesn't mean change comes in a heck of a hurry. I was told that I had no rights. I was told you'll never get married, well today I'm happily married. I live in a place of my own, I have a job I enjoy doing. And yes we have, well, we call her our child, our cat, because we don't have any children. But boy is she spoiled. My wife says "We've got to spoil something, we've got no kids."

That's the big void in my life, is the fact that we don't have children. I would have liked children. But it's just one of those things. At that time, I didn't know. I wish I knew what People First has taught me back twenty-one years ago. However, I didn't. Life goes on. Let's look toward the future.

Patrick: Did you decide you didn't want kids?

Peter: Well, we talked about it. At that time I was on the road an average of three weekends a month. So she said I wouldn't be home often enough when the kids are growing up, and I said that's true. And there were a few other reasons. Anyhow, we didn't have them, and now we wish we did. Hindsight is twenty-twenty.

Patrick: Aren't you like a parent of People First?

Peter: In my life, I wanted to become a minister. Now, my ministry is People First. The movement has come a long ways since I didn't know what I was doing.

Empowerment and the architecture of rights based social policy

Tim Stainton

Empowerment has for a decade or more been a keyword in social work and other human services. While definitions vary, the essence of empowerment is about enhancing, securing and/or legitimating the power of oneself, another, or a collective. For people who have been labelled as having a learning disability this is indeed a profound change – and challenge – to a society and service system which have on many occasions either inadvertently or actively sought to diminish, delegitimate, oppress and control those so labelled (see Macnicol, 1989; Stainton, 1998a; Thomson, 1998). The related ideas of rights, choice, citizenship and self-determination have now become well established as a philosophy or value base said to underlie progressive policy and services for people with a learning disability (see DoH, 2001; MCFD, 2002). Exactly what this means in practice and the theoretical imperatives underlying it, however, are somewhat less clear.

This article will consider what these ideas imply in the way of structures and policy and will argue that a coherent model is emerging with recognizable elements. Examples are drawn primarily from the UK and British Columbia, Canada to illustrate the changes. The article will then look at some of the issues related to successful implementation of a rights or empowerment based model of policy and structures for supporting people labelled as having a learning disability. The article begins with a brief discussion of some background and theoretical issues.

Empowerment, rights and self-determination

One commonality underlying most current changes in policy and practice is a move away from a paternalistic model, where *we* decided "what was best for these people", assuming *they* were incapable of making choices, or at least "good" choices. Indeed, current initiatives emphasize choice as a central feature of progressive systems. Initially the emphasis has been on eliminating barriers to participation and providing some broad legal protection to citizens with learning and other disabilities. By the 1980s we began to see explicit protection for people with learning disabilities in legal instruments. Notable is the inclusion of "mental disability" within the Canadian Charter of Rights and Freedoms in 1982 which afforded equal protection against discrimination, and the Americans with Disabilities Act of 1990.

Similar legislation is now in place to varying degrees in numerous jurisdictions including the UK with the Disability Discrimination Act 1995. These are significant achievements and have been effective in offering protection against everything from involuntary sterilization, unfair discrimination at work and the denial of the right to vote, medical treatment or educational opportunities, though effectiveness varies across jurisdictions.

While these fundamental protections have to a lesser degree provided the positive supports necessary for the exercise of citizenship, their impact has been largely in the area of protection against discrimination. What is less clear is how policy structures and instruments needed to change to support the empowerment of individuals to exercise their rights and citizenship. In essence, the question is: "What is the architecture for rights or empowerment based policy?"

While it is not possible in the current article to examine the detailed theoretical underpinnings of such an approach, a few comments will help to set the stage for a more detailed examination of the specific policy elements (for a detailed examination of the theoretical issues see Stainton, 1994). Two critical assumptions when considering how we approach the question of policy and structure from an empowerment or rights' perspective help to distinguish it from previous approaches. First, we are concerned with *capacity* not outcome. That is, we are concerned with how choices are made, not what choice is made. In service terms this is why self-determination or rights based approaches focus on ways of supporting choice making such as advocacy and independent planning, not on programmes such as vocational or residential services.

Second, we are interested not only in the act of deciding what a person wants to do, but also with their ability to act on that choice. Telling someone they are free to decide to go to a mainstream school but not providing the means for them to act on that choice is no choice at all. This emphasis on *capacity* not *outcome* is in my view a critical difference between a rights based approach and other approaches to policy and practice in this area.

One further issue concerns equality. The problem is sometimes called the "difference dilemma", and refers to the problem that what people require to achieve an equal citizenship differs with each individual. In other words "equal treatment" does equate with equal citizenship since different people require different types of treatment to achieve the same basic capacity for participation. For example, a person who cannot use her legs requires different means to achieve basic mobility than does someone who walks. Being concerned with *equal capacity* requires *differential treatment based on differential needs* to achieve the *same relative capacity* for participation and citizenship.

While the example above may be relatively easy to deal with, this dilemma becomes more acute as the nature and complexity of needs increase. This complexity makes it impossible to establish general universal provisions which will satisfy all individuals' needs. The challenge then for social policy is not to find better services, but to create a structure in which individuals can articulate their demands directly and which allows the state to adjudicate and meet legitimate claims in a manner which does not in itself infringe the person's potential participation. In essence, what is required is a structure within which an ongoing dialogue on legitimate claims can occur between the individual and the state, as the representative of the collective (Stainton, 1994).

Elements of a rights based social policy

The key elements of such a structure are, I suggest, now fairly clear, with most elements having been implemented to one degree or another in a large number of jurisdictions. They include three key elements which have been previously described (Stainton, 1994):

- support for people to articulate their claims

- support for people to identify, obtain and manage supports necessary to actualize their claims

- providing control over the resources.

A fourth element which has more recently emerged is concerned with *governance:* that is, issues of who controls decision making within the system, not simply on an individual level, but on a broader structural level. I will briefly consider each of the above and then return to the question of an integrated structure to support the empowerment and rights of people with a learning disability and some of the current challenges of implementation.

Support for people to articulate their claims

The logic of this element is pretty straight forward. If people are to be empowered to control their own lives then they need to be able to articulate their wants, needs and choices. For many people with a learning disability this can be problematic, either because they do not use formal communication methods, or because their voice is suppressed through laws which declare them incompetent, through services which do not listen, or through having been denied the chance to develop self-advocacy skills. The increase in advocacy is one example of how this element has begun to be more formally recognized and incorporated into policy and structures. The advocacy commitment and investment in the UK learning disability strategy *Valuing People* (DoH, 2001) is a good example; the Australian Advocacy Commission is another.

While governments have been increasingly recognizing and supporting advocacy, including self-advocacy, they have been less keen to recognize the rights of advocates to the tools needed to represent effectively the interests of those they advocate for. Stories of advocates being excluded or challenged by those in authority are fairly common when issues become difficult. The 1986 Disabled Person (Representation and Consultation) Act did contain provisions for personal representatives and gave them equal rights of access to information and participation as the individual. This, however, was scrapped by the government before implementation, and some 18 years later no similar provision has since been put into place.

This leads into more formal arrangements for supporting decision making. Many jurisdictions have been concerned with reforming their guardianship and related laws to provide options which do not involve an automatic loss of rights. Several Canadian jurisdictions have recognized the need for independent personal representation to be recognized in law.

Current initiatives in British Columbia call for the status of personal networks to be recognized in law (MCFD, 2002).

One of the most progressive pieces of legislation in this area is British Columbia's Representation Agreement Act 1996 which provides a simple, inexpensive means for individuals to formally recognize one or more persons as their representatives for routine health, personal care, financial decision making and legal affairs. The real innovation in this Act is its change to the way capacity is viewed and understood. Rather than a simple common law test of capacity to determine whether one can formally express an understanding of the meaning and consequences of a given decision, the Act relies on expanding the traditional concepts around communication and the nature and quality of the relationship. Section 3 (2) notes that "An adult's way of communicating with others is not grounds for deciding that he or she is incapable of understanding anything referred to in subsection (1)". Section 8 of the Act states:

> (1) An adult may make a representation agreement... even though the adult is incapable of
>
> a) making a contract; or
>
> (b) managing his or her health care, personal care, legal matters, financial affairs, business or assets.
>
> (2) In deciding whether an adult is incapable of making a representation agreement ...all relevant factors must be considered, for example:
>
> (a) whether the adult communicates a desire to have a representative make, help make, or stop making decisions;
>
> (b) whether the adult demonstrates choices and preferences and can express feelings of approval or disapproval of others;
>
> (c) whether the adult is aware that making the

representation agreement or changing or revoking any of the provisions means that the representative may make, or stop making, decisions or choices that affect the adult;

(d) whether there is a relationship with the representative that is characterized by trust.

The three key shifts which are required are an expanded notion of communication; an emphasis on the quality of the relationship (trust) between persons, so that when people may not be able to traditionally communicate their choices, those best placed to interpret for them, i.e. those who know them best, are empowered to represent them; and recognition that incapacity is often a function of lack of support rather than inherent in the person. This is essential for individuals who cannot directly articulate their wants and needs if they are to avoid having their needs solely determined by professionals or legal guardians who have little knowledge of who they are as individuals and whose interest in them is professional rather than personal.

The difficulty of shifting this long standing legal notion of capacity can be witnessed in the long and tortuous road of UK attempts to reform their guardianship and related laws (see Law Commission, 1995; Lord Chancellor's Department, 1997; 1999). Begun in 1995, at the time of writing a new law is still not in place and the recent Bill (Secretary of State for Constitutional Affairs, 2003) falls far short of the type of reforms required to meet the criteria discussed above. The Attorney General of British Columbia (2004) has also tried recently to replace the Representation Agreement Act but was halted by strong community advocacy from seniors and disability groups.

While advocacy and representation are not new concepts, what is new from a public policy perspective is that the state is increasingly recognizing the structural necessity of independent support for articulating wants and needs and the importance of unpaid personally bonded and committed individuals in the lives of people with learning disabilities. Traditional ideas about competence and capacity are, however, proving difficult to reverse.

Support for people to identify, obtain and manage supports necessary to actualize their claims

Related to the above is the second element: the necessity of independent support to assist people to identify, obtain and manage supports necessary to act on their choices. The increasing centrality of independent personal planning support and coordination for people with learning disabilities reflects this imperative to support people to not only identify but also actively pursue and manage their supports. The emphasis on person centred planning in *Valuing People* (DoH, 2001) is one such example. Western Australia's local area coordination (SCRCSSP, 1998) is another example. Independent planning and support is also a central feature of current reforms in British Columbia (MCFD, 2002). While planning models and support systems such as service brokerage have been around for decades (Salisbury et al., 1987), the key issue, as with the first element, is integration into the system rather than an add-on or an approach pursued by a few progressive people or organizations.

One aspect of this that is less well understood is what is meant by "independent". While most would agree to the benefit of person centred planning and ongoing support, a key structural element is often ignored, namely, the location of the planning agent. Too often the organization planning support is also responsible for the funding or service delivery, placing them in a conflict of interest position. This often results in either a service led approach (Stainton, 1998b) or a lack of well funded, ongoing planning supports being available to individuals and families. A key feature of the proposed approach to the British Columbia model is a strict separation between the personal planning element and the service and funding responsibilities, along with an ongoing right of access to planning support for individuals and families (MCFD, 2002). The value of independent planning support has been confirmed in several studies of UK direct payments projects where independent support provided by disabled people themselves has been highly valued by consumers (Stainton and Boyce, 2004).

Providing control over the resources

The third element of this emerging architecture is the increasingly common use of individualized funding (IF) or direct payments (DP) as a means to ensure control over resources remains with individuals rather than with services or systems (Lord and Hutchison, 2003; MCFD, 2002; SCRCSSP, 1998). The UK direct payments programme is a good example of a comprehensive model integrated into the mainstream social service system. The logic here, simply put, is that if people are receiving resources from the state as a matter of right, then they should have the right to control how the resources are used to meet the agreed needs. There is also an increasingly strong body of research evidence to support the claim that IF/DP enhances both the control individuals and families feel over their own lives and the effectiveness of the support (Dawson, 2000; Lord and Hutchison, 2003; Powers et al., 2003; Rosenau, 2002; Stainton and Boyce, 2004).

Governance

As noted above, governance is increasingly becoming part of the discussion on human service reform. Often not in so many words, but concern with who is involved in decision making about policy, funding distribution and community planning is frequently part of policy reform in the area. This is the macro level equivalent to direct funding and individual planning. The partnership boards that are part of the *Valuing People* initiative are one such example. On a slightly smaller but more radical scale, the increasing centrality of consumer controlled and directed organizations in the implementation of direct payments in the UK is another example (Hasler et al., 1999; Stainton and Boyce, 2004). This goes one step further than "partnership", and emphasizes the point that those who are best informed about how disability related policy and services are delivered are disabled people themselves and their families. Current reforms in British Columbia called for almost the entire community living service division, with an approximate annual budget of $604 million Cdn, to be turned over to a community based board with a legislated mandatory majority of self-advocates and family members (MCFD, 2002). Although the government has baulked at mandated self-advocate representatives, once again arguing "capability", they have agreed to a majority of members with a strong personal connection to community living (British Columbia, 2004).

While the state rightfully remains responsible for ensuring taxpayer monies are spent prudently and with reasonable fiscal controls, the notion of governance recognizes that once a legitimate interest or claim is established, those most directly involved in that claim have a further right to determine how best to meet the needs inherent in that claim. As noted above, this is simply the same logic as IF/DP, but on a macro level. It remains to be seen just how far beyond "partnership", which is usually a partnership on government terms, states are prepared to go.

Impediments and direction

As the above indicates, all the elements of a rights based architecture for policy are now relatively commonplace. There are, however, several factors which are inhibiting an effective rights based system from emerging:

- Lack of coordination of the elements into a coherent system.

- Lack of sufficient independence of the elements. For example, in many jurisdictions it is still the fund holders who also support planning and/or provide services, which is a clear conflict of interest.

- Piecemeal or add-on approaches which impair the overall integrity of the system.

- Many jurisdictions have introduced a single element without the others, which in many cases reduces or eliminates their effectiveness as instruments to foster equal citizenship.

A good example of how the three elements, when not in concert, can impede progress is the experience of people with a learning disability and direct payments in the UK. The requirement that users must be able to consent to and manage direct payments has been a major stumbling block for people with a learning disability in trying to access direct payments (DoH, 2001; Glasby and Littlechild, 2002). While efforts are currently being made to increase their participation through better guidance to local authorities (DoH, 2004) and proposed changes to the law on capacity, as discussed above, these changes at present do not seem to go far enough to allow comprehensive access to those with a broad range of learning disabilities. The key point here is that when all three elements are present and integrated, the likelihood of true empowerment, participation and meaningful citizenship is increased exponentially. When elements are introduced in an unsystematic or inconsistent manner, the overall effect on empowerment will be seriously compromised.

Conclusion

This article has briefly outlined the key elements of a policy approach and structure which can support the empowerment of people with a learning disability. It is not a panacea, nor is it a complete answer to the question of how best we can support the full inclusion and citizenship of people with a learning disability. This article has, however, outlined an architecture for support which is emerging in many jurisdictions, and which, when fully and properly implemented, will create an environment for individuals to fulfil their citizenship aspirations as equal people first.

What Remains Worth Struggling For

Michael Kendrick

The Inevitability Of Struggle

There is a wish in all of us that life be not so taxing and difficult. We resist the idea of making something as seemingly dire, as struggle often is, to be anything but an exception to the norm. The thought that life could be equated with struggle is abhorrent to our modern belief that suffering of all kinds ought to be entirely escapable. Perhaps we no longer appreciate that our ancestors would be utterly puzzled by the idea of the world being a site for perfect happiness. Curiously, many of them would have said after some reflection, that they actually became happier when they came to accept the struggles of life rather than to run from them. We are pulled in many directions by the prospects of struggle, and finding how to manage it will rest, to a great extent, upon what we believe about the inevitability of struggle.

If, for instance, we believe that struggle is harmful to us, then it is quite logical to avoid it, and to disparage taking up any challenge that might result in strife, tribulation or frustration. Yet if this belief were to be pursued with any consistency, only easy problems would ever be faced, and the admirable strengths that arise at times of great human struggle might well be lost from sight. There would be no incentive to exercise courage, to seek or inspire idealism, to show solidarity with other people, or to commit acts of great virtue. We would lack edifying role models, and most certainly would be deprived of the excitement and spiritual uplift that comes from witnessing the good that people can do when it is important enough.

At the same time, not all versions of struggle are ennobling, and it is important not to lose sight of the many ways in which struggles can result in misery, tedium and depression. Struggle is, in many ways, a paradox: it is changed in its outcomes through the way that it is perceived and taken up by each participant. In this respect, struggle is a fundamental human experience, and is thus changed by the human orientation towards it. For example, it is obvious that there is much struggle in preparing for, and running a marathon race, yet for many dedicated runners, a marathon may well be a deeply meaningful or mystical experience. It is also possible that the experience of being in a marathon may strike the unenthused as being a form of torture.

The essential point to grasp is that struggle is integral to the accomplishment of many things in life, and may not be avoidable as a practical matter. Similarly, how one views struggle is not fixed, as there is usually a wide range of responses to a specific struggle, and how it is viewed and managed. An additional point to consider is that not all approaches to struggle are the same in terms of either the benefits or the personal costs of taking up a specific struggle. This suggests that there is always a need to evaluate the question of struggle, and this discretion raises the further question of whether there is an accumulated wisdom that one can rely on in regard to how struggle might best be managed.

Making Peace With The Inevitability Of Struggle

It has already been observed that people will take on demanding struggles, and may even seem to enjoy them. For instance, parents will often tell of the many struggles that their children have caused them, yet conclude that having children is the best thing they have ever done. It has all been worthwhile for them despite the deprivations and personal toll that has come with making a commitment to their children. Few people would say that their lives have been endlessly satisfying, but many would say that the experience has had its share of joy. Clearly, it is possible to make peace with struggles, or at least with some of them.

Some of the conventional advice that one might receive on coming to terms with struggle is worth remembering, because it has a long lineage in the common experience of many people. For instance, it is commonly said that we should try to "pick our struggles". This often means that the struggles that we have taken on, consciously and freely, are easier to bear than those that are imposed on us. It also suggests that some struggles are not suited to us, and we would be wise to evaluate the struggles that have the right fit with our lives, capacities, and motivations. In other words, there might well be valid struggles that ought to be taken up by someone, but not necessarily by us. Conceivably, some struggles might so damage and devastate us that there is ample wisdom in avoiding them.

Some struggles may simply lack meaning and purpose for

us, though they may well interest and motivate others. In this regard we may feel a certain "calling" to some challenges, yet lack that feeling in regard to other struggles. This may not be a case of the inherent merit of a specific struggle so much as it is a measure of its fit with our own unique life purposes. This is often evident in the unconventional nature of the life-callings of some individuals, as well as the extent to which many people are deeply content with the conventionality of their lives and struggles. The term, "each to their own", is an expression of this wisdom.

A more elusive challenge is posed by the problem of adversity. It is one thing to work towards selectively taking up our own personal struggles, but it is another to have struggles descend on us unbidden. Adversity need not be seen as unnatural, though when it is, the temptation would be to see oneself as a victim of misfortune, and perhaps even the target of malignant forces of some kind. In some cases, a person might feel helpless or irreparably damaged in the face of a catastrophe, and this sense may never leave the person who is traumatised by misfortune.

Alternatively, one can sometimes gradually suspend judgement about the underlying character of adversity, and resolve to await the insights that time might provide regarding the ultimate meaning of an adversity. In this regard, unsolicited adversity, as an aspect of struggle, can be managed just as voluntary struggles can be. There are many people who will attest to the unexpected or hidden benefits of adversity, though such adversity was never sought. Rather, the person involved gradually came to see the adversity in a new light. Knowing that this shift is possible can often open up people to new prospects.

Moving towards reconciliation with the struggles that one faces, or has chosen, normally involves a willingness to sacrifice, and to maintain the kind of commitment that ensures that the struggle will be meaningful. For instance, if the nature of a struggle that a person had resolved to manage, were a decision to care for a parent who had suddenly become dependent, then that commitment would most likely mean the foregoing of many desirable things that the person would have done were it not for the new responsibility. In addition, the person may well be taking up new, and possibly unattractive duties, which are related to supporting the dependent person. This combination of sacrifice and commitment might well come easily to some people, but for others it may be a substantial struggle, particularly if there are tasks or sacrifices involved that are alien to, or uncomfortable for, the person who is taking up the struggle.

The ways of reaching peace with one's struggles are too personal, existential and specific, to be reduced to a formula. On the contrary, it is a quintessentially human task to decide one's path in life, including which struggles to take up and which ones to let go. "Mindfulness" is much closer to what should be aspired to, rather than to proceed by imitating others, or by following only well-travelled paths. The struggle is a burden in its way, but it is also an opportunity to regain the direction of our lives again and again, as we confront our struggles and guide them to resolution.

Reflecting On Where The Struggle Is Located

The culture in which we live helps to shape us both inwardly and outwardly, giving us values, priorities and views of our world, that orient us to what is important and fundamental about our lives. Cultures are not infallible in this regard, and often mislead us about what is good and worthy. Cultural beliefs and values influence how we approach our struggles, and in the process, provide us with ways in which we evaluate how we are doing. For instance, in a materialist culture, such as our own, the acquisition of physical comfort, possessions and other forms of material wealth may well provide many people with a sense of what the "good life" is. Yet, if we reject these as measures of a "good life", then the struggle we may face might be one of being culturally marginalised, at least as it relates to the primacy of materialism.

In relation to where we locate problems and solutions, we are also guided by our culture. In an externalised culture such as our own, which exalts the tangible world that can be objectified, measured, quantified and manipulated, it should come as no surprise that we are often biased towards seeing problems as being located "out there, in the world", and apart from ourselves. Naturally, if we see the problem as "out there", then that is exactly where we will solve it. If, on the other hand, we see ourselves as part of the world, subjective, partially-invisible and not solely our material being, then we will look for solutions that are "in here", involving our own consciousness and personal values, and will draw upon remedies that are not simply material in character.

In this regard, there may be problems that surface "out there" in our visible world, that have their origins inside people, and arise from what is going on with their inner life. Anger, despair and a sense of hopelessness about justice may well fuel desperate actions by deprived people. Yet, on another level, the conditions in the world that have produced these perceptions may, in turn, have arisen out of the inner life of people who have created a social order that favours them, even as it disadvantages others. Each is creating an effect on others "out there", whether they realise it or not. Nevertheless, remedies solely focussed "out there", and cut off from authentic personal changes "in here", may well create unhelpful results given the fundamental origins of the difficulties.

This logic would illustrate why it is dangerous to impose our view of reform and remedies on other people, as it may well construct goals and obligations for others while leaving ourselves untouched. This is not an abstruse point lacking practicality, as there is not only an element of hypocrisy in burdening others with responsibilities that are more properly our own, but there is also the unconscious disengagement of people from the effects they are creating in the world. When we are right, and everyone else is wrong, is it any wonder that they can never be right. Equally, when we are willing to be engaged about our place in the world, then it becomes possible to be effective in that world.

This paradox can be seen in the subtle distinctions between whether the world needs "more" or "better" by way of a class of solutions. The former is normally a quantitative term, and the latter a qualitative one. For instance, is the poverty of so many people in our world to be solved by simply having more, or will it also require that we all be better people? Is the poverty of people simply because they have less, or is it partially relational, in that others have more because they are favoured by the social or economic order? If the answer is that poverty has nothing to do with the conduct of the favoured, then the poor have only to be inventive about getting more. If, on the other hand, poverty could be seen more as a societal phenomenon, then another class of solutions opens up that may require us to be "better" people, and to subsequently do "more" of some particular things.

Many of us are instinctively drawn to the impulse that if we just had more, then much would be achieved. We often long for more money, more people, more interest, more programs, more power, more time, more support, more expertise, more science and so on. We are not deluded in this regard, as many of these could be beneficial. However, we need to consider the further question of what the origins of "more" are, at their core, and how this might be mobilised. Without a commensurate interest in the question of people struggling to be "better", then good outcomes are unlikely to materialise from their invisible inner recesses within people. "More" and "better" are both dependent on what is, or is not, happening within people. If the assumption is that there is at least some good in people, then it may not be too farfetched to strengthen this idea and to resist its dilution.

Not surprisingly, poverty would be altered considerably by the strategy of people asking themselves how they could be better in relation to others, as well as by the poor and the privileged alike committing themselves to doing more of what is available for them to do. The poor solely blaming the rich for their misery may be as unproductive as the rich blaming the poor for their circumstances. However, when both the poor and the rich want to see their own part in the problem, the problem then becomes one "in here" for both groups, thereby making its eventual resolution more probable, conscious and potentially just.

Recognising how we set up problems and solutions does not resolve the fact that we need wisdom in our choice of the values that guide our conduct. However, this recognition does let us see that we all face problems regarding our own authenticity and our need to be "better". It may also help us to want to know others, and to understand what makes them work. If we can work together, and build some measure of commonality, them many problems "out there" may yield, by degree, to our collective efforts. On the other hand, there can be no collective efforts unless there are first some personal inward changes, in all of us, in terms of our willingness to relate to others. Our collective progress inches forward only to the extent that each of us sincerely works to be a better person.

Examples Of Struggles That Still Await Our Further Commitment

As long as there is such a thing as "we", there will be prospects for shared struggles of all kinds. The needs of human beings are so persistent and diverse, that we are constantly confronted by circumstances that are compelling. The merit of a struggle is not in its prominence or scale, but rather in the ways in which it draws upon us to be our best. There are many such struggles, at this point in time, which remain as relevant now as they were in other periods of our history. It is important to appreciate their universality, as well as to note with gratitude the contributions of those who came before us, making it possible for us to achieve the results we can garner today.

Values, Ideology And The Dignity Of The Person

It has been a recurring theme in the struggles of people with disabilities, and their allies, that they have had to make relentless efforts to have their humanity fully recognised and appreciated. This is true today in that we all still hold stereotypes about people with disabilities that are dehumanising, diminishing of their personhood, and often harmful because they cast people into devalued social roles. While it is true that the overt nature of this kind of abuse might be less acute than at other times in history, the negative messages are often muted, rather than eliminated. At the heart of this kind of abuse is the preference, which we all harbour, for seeing people as somehow "less than" ourselves. Although our actions and beliefs might be unconscious, this does not mean that they are unnoticed or without effect. On the contrary, those who are treated in this way are exquisitely sensitive to how they are perceived and valued. One only has to ask people with disabilities to share their stories, to hear distressing vignettes about how many people still behave towards them.

Nonetheless, gradual progress has been made in countless small ways, mainly because we have become more attuned to the way that our attitudes influence our behaviour and patterns of life. Through different kinds of consciousness-raising we have been helped us see people as they actually are – as people rather than as socially distant categories or objects. This, in turn, has helped to break down barriers so that it is somewhat more likely we will see a person as being unique, with the many strengths and shortcomings that beset all of us.

Respecting The Voices Of People

It is puzzling to see how often decisions are made for people with disabilities rather than with them. This suggests that many of us still do not recognise that we need to fundamentally change our behaviour so that what people with disabilities want and need is determined by, and with, them. Although we might mean well in our actions that take over people's lives, this still results in conduct that most people would find offensive and paternalistic. Worse yet, we structure this paternalism into habitual and institutionalised patterns that leave people with disabilities dis-empowered and hostage to the whims of others. It is ironic that we do this whilst undeniably believing that we are essentially showing respect to those people.

Such an obvious violation of how people ought to be treated gives greater urgency to the question of whether we are truly in "right relationship" with people who have disabilities; as long as we are still seeking "right relationship", there is always the hope that we can eventually do better. However, we cannot let our voices grow so loud that the voices of people with disabilities go unheeded or need to be loud and angry to be heard. We need to be quiet and small enough so that even voices that are merely a whisper can be heard. Occasionally there is a tendency to see the solution as making the voices of people with disabilities louder, confrontational, and more aggressive, which may be an imposition, of a style that is not their own on many individuals.

A simpler answer would be to let the "voice" of people with disabilities be what it actually is, in all its diversity. A wealth of different people and voices lies behind our broad labels, and we are going to have our work cut out for us if we are to redouble our efforts and listen to people, with the right spirit.

Supporting The Supporters

Few people would quarrel with the assertion that family and friends still remain the most dependable form of social support for people with disabilities. While we have attempted to substitute for these natural supports with paid human services, few people are satisfied with the outcome. This is for good reason, as most people recognise and value the special qualities of concern and commitment that come from people who love them, as opposed to people for whom it is a job.

Perhaps it is because we have placed so much energy during the last decades into building up formal systems of support, that we have lost sight of the more fundamental role and contribution of informal supporters. The service system now consumes proportionately more resources than those that go to nourish and support families and friendships. One only has to look at spending levels on family-support to see where the real priority is. Unless families go into acute crisis, they may be neglected. We are much better at getting people into formalised professional services than we are at supporting them through their natural networks, even though their families and friends may be the only ones who have shown a lifetime of commitment to them.

It is not clear how we might do better in this regard, because simply spending more money on families and other natural supporters may have the unintended consequence of turning families and friends into "de facto" staff. Nonetheless, it should be assumed that we would eventually make progress on this question of supporting the natural supporters, if we turn our attention to it. We may have to learn that many natural supporters should be seen as potential innovators, allies for change, and advocates, if we are to begin to more fully grasp how this potential could be better husbanded. When natural supporters become a more fundamental part of discussions about what is a better way of doing things, then surely they will be properly recognised and respected.

The Need For Moral And Principled Leaders

It has always been true that we have needed leaders who have coaxed us towards discovering the directions that would result in real progress. We will always need leaders who not only effectively lead us in the right direction, but who also do so with integrity. Such leaders are not going to appear just because they are needed, and naturally, they will pass with each generation. Not only must we identify, recruit and orient new leaders but we must also show concern for keeping our present leaders renewed, relevant and challenged. Many people think of emergent leaders as simply being restricted to people who gain titles, but this is deeply mistaken, because leadership can come from any social group including people with disabilities, their families, employers, bureaucrats, academics, or ordinary members of the community, given any issue and the people who might step forward to act on them.

What may need to be appreciated is that we can either assume that such leaders will magically appear just because we need them, or we can take a more prudent course and proactively identify, recruit, develop, support and renew potential leaders long before they are needed. We can see this need now, as a whole generation is preparing to pass from the disability field. So little has been done to prepare the upcoming generation for the leadership challenges that they will inherit from the present generation. Without the catalytic presence of a new generation of principled leaders, it is predictable that other influences will enter this leadership vacuum. Perhaps some of those influences may turn out to be benign or even progressive, but it is useful to consider what may be lost if they are not. We have struggled hard for our values and for the reforms that they have brought about – it would be a pity if these were left undefended through the absence of leaders who are able to recognise and appreciate their importance.

People Who Will Take The Hard Stand

There are always times when it is important to have people who will stand on principle, and challenge society to live up to its better nature and traditions. Such activists may be formal or informal, local or national, prominent or obscure, but they will be known by their willingness to embrace the crucial issues that must be faced, and do so in ways that go to the heart of issues. It is an often-quoted observation that one person can save a city, and so we are not talking about a great mass of activists, as much as we are about the presence of activists and advocates of great distinction, principle, and vision.

In the case of moral leaders, our prospects for having principled people are increased if we lay the seeds for their formation and maturation well in advance of the times of tribulation in which their courage, vision and character will be most needed. While it is true that such people are fundamentally born, not made, it is also true that these natural gifts are more likely to come into play when they are recognised, valued and supported so that they develop to the higher levels of their potential. If we are to have social movements that are vigorous, challenging and positive, we will need advocates who will act as the stimulus for such movements. Taking the trouble to ensure that strong advocates will be there when they are needed is clearly worthy of struggle.

Service Structures Inspired By "Right Relationship"

The chaos of our modern service systems is all too evident to the people who rely on them and who have to work in them. Despite our best intentions and the application of vast resources, these systems are very difficult to keep on the right path. When they lose their way, it can mean the rupture of positive relationships between services and the people they serve. A breakdown in the ethical foundations of the relationship between services and those they assist will undoubtedly require a great deal of thoughtful action to build, and rebuild.

It is not that such ethical relationships cannot exist, as there are innumerable instances where these relationships are wholesome or even inspiring, however, the scale, complexity and powerful vested-interests in these systems provide huge obstacles for keeping the proper alignments, which will be needed to meet the test of right and honourable relationships. It can be anticipated that keeping such systems honest, whether from the inside or the outside, will provide committed change-agents with ample opportunities for struggling with the many issues that are involved.

Improved Theory And Practice

It is worrying that we hear so many complaints about the quality of community services, given how hard it has been to get them established to a point where they might become a more reliable resource for people with disabilities and their families than formal service systems. At the same time, these complaints and dissatisfactions can guide us to where further work is needed, or where our theory about practice needs to be revised. It is always painful to have our contributions criticised, but we can draw important insights into how we might do better by attending to the lessons that lie behind the criticisms. The reality is that we need to keep evolving, and that many of our service models, and the theories behind them, are increasingly out-of-date.

Some hope can be drawn from the fact that our potential for learning today is as strong as it has always been. In addition, we have witnessed all sorts of advances in the past four decades, in both our thinking and practice. The state of the art has noticeably improved on many aspects of service. Nevertheless, potential of this kind alone does not do the job. We need people who will harness the potential, so that people's lives are changed for the better through their contact with services. In fact, we need a whole new generation of people who see their mission as being a fundamental assault on all the reasons why human services have not been of good quality. Naturally, this is an intimidating prospect, but not beyond our grasp.

Strengthening People's Ability To Innovate Usefully

It is obvious that many people have the capacity to innovate, but are blocked from doing so, by their own limitations, and by the many discouragements that may be present in the environments that they have to contend with. It is also obvious that innovation is not a kind of fixed-outcome, but has a more variable character. With the proper stimulations and support, a surprising number of people can participate meaningfully in formulating, and negotiating into reality, many striking innovations. We will always need creative people and supportive settings that foster innovation. We will also need the allies of innovation, who can provide the kind of political and situational leadership that permits innovations to be to be conceived and helped to reach the practical maturity of their inherent potential.

These innovators, and the constellations of like-minded people in the process of change, are not random in their occurrence, and it is possible to deliberately envision and nurture them. Doing so is quite a struggle, but there are strategies that can be thoughtfully applied, accelerating the likelihood of successful innovation.

Relationships And Social Belonging

It is common to hear people speak of the value of social inclusion, although it was not so long ago that support for the segregation of people with disabilities was widespread. This is encouraging because it shows what can be done when people go deep enough into change that long-term habits such as patterned social exclusion fade from prominence. This does not mean that we do not have problems of this kind now, as we can see that people with disabilities are still not welcomed whole-heartedly, that many lack the kind of sincere personal relationships that they need, and that they simply do not seem to have a valued place in many aspects of our community. These are crucial thresholds that we must move beyond collectively and individually. In fact, each of us would be well advised to actually live social inclusion better, rather than concentrating on exhorting services to do better on this issue.

This will begin to happen when we are helped to see the need for each of us to be personally present for people with disabilities when it comes to real relationships. People with disabilities need to become more a genuine part of our personal and intimate lives, even while they might still remain only legally tolerated in public life. We do not need to be "perfect" in our relationships, as that kind of pretence would be unhelpful. Instead, relationships, and the character of social and personal presence must be authentic, unfeigned and hopefully enjoyable. So we face the twin challenges of "more" social inclusion and "better" social inclusion; we must successfully face the inner challenges of social inclusion as well as the outer ones. Neither has been easy thus far, so it can be assumed that this next stage will be a struggle.

People With Disabilities And Their Positive Contributions To Our Lives and Communities

It is quite one-sided to dwell unduly on the neediness, deficiencies and problems that are faced by people with disabilities without giving balance through an appreciation of the actual and potential contributions made everyday to us, as individuals, and to our communities. These contributions are often exciting, beneficial and worthy of much credit. If we never draw attention to these contributions we might walk right past many accomplishments as if they did not matter. By concentrating so much on what people have difficulty doing, we will miss what they are doing that is of value, and of knowing what people want to do with their lives.

The stereotypical attitudes that we have undoubtedly make non-disabled people feel good about themselves, at the price of masking the goodness and virtues of people with disabilities. By using them to feed our own psychic needs, we may find that the potential virtues of non-disabled people become "deformed" by our own neediness. The obvious solution for this is to re-dedicate ourselves to the task of recognising goodness wherever we find it, and being sure that our celebration of virtue is fairer to individuals whose disability overshadows the real identity of the person. In this regard, to be able to receive what is given may be just as important as to give what is needed.

Conclusion

There are still many worthwhile struggles that would ask the best of us, and provide us with much satisfaction along with the difficulties. Struggles ask much of us, including a willingness to be found wanting and to fail at things that we care much about. It is safer, in many ways, to walk away from struggles, as we will never have to take painful risks. Even so, being personally safe may not be the highest value, nor may it be where we find the most authenticity and satisfaction in our lives. To struggle may well be the only way we can grow and develop, and it would be a pity to turn away from our potential because of what struggle requires of us. As we have seen in this exploration, the inner struggles are the most defining ones.

Centering Our Planning
On People

Judith A. Snow

In the early "80"s something surprising began to happen. People set about designing ways to create plans with individuals who have some sort of disability label. This new type of plan was focused on one person only - an almost extravagant idea.

People started to do workshops to teach such planning and share new techniques and insights. I attended just such an event in 1983. It took place over an entire week. We examined the activities that usually occupied us - as busy working adults - throughout a day, a week and a year. We experimented with planning a similarly full day, week and year with some people who were living in group homes. It was exciting to realize that people could break out of isolated, boring situations and, with the right supports, be active participants in the communities around them.

By the end of the 90's the available selection of planning processes ranged from quick and easy to implement through to comprehensive and intricate techniques. Person Centred Planning had become a distinctive and rich approach to supporting people who are labeled disabled. Many, many stories accumulated showing how useful such planning is when friends, families and service providers aim to support a vulnerable person to participate as an ordinary citizen with other citizens in ordinary places.

The activities we call Person Centred Planning were inconceivable forty five years ago. Today's widespread adoption of Person Centred Planning marks a deep shift in our culture. A welcome change is taking place in how we view people, diversity and ability.

The first aspect of this cultural shift is that there is a growing appreciation of the personhood of a person who has been labeled disabled. This has not always been the case. Throughout history - and too often today - people with mental, physical or emotional challenges were and are viewed as something other than human.

What do others see in you when they recognize that you are a person? They see many things, of course, but three things are fundamental. First, people see that you can play a significant role in the economy - the rich network of activities that gets things done in our communities. As economic participants people create and produce things, pass along information, buy and sell goods and services, form formal and informal work teams, hold down jobs, employ others and make demands on "the market".

Secondly, when people see that you are a person they see that you are responsible. Responsible people set the course of their lives, make choices, carry out decisions, solve problems, ask questions, make judgments, seek out better information and resources, hone their skills, and reliably support other people's participation.

Thirdly, a person builds and sustains relationships. People typically have a wide range of family, friend, casual, work, neighbourhood, close and distant relationships. Most people know hundreds of other people. Being in relationship is a core experience for human beings. We define our identities in terms of these connections. People expect people to enter into and sustain a wide variety of relationships.

If someone falls short in one or more of these areas of economic participation, responsibility and relationship then people could use this as evidence that they are not a person. People with disability labels typically are jobless and play few or no roles in the economy except to "consume" services. They rarely carry out responsible roles, and frequently are extensively supervised - by educational assistants, case managers, social workers and more. People who are labeled disabled also typically experience isolation. They nearly always know fewer people than their typical counterparts, and the relationships they do have are shaped to a large degree by the human service system. So instead of knowing and contributing to a broad range of people based on interest, neighbourhood, employment, family and history, labeled folk usually know and contribute to a smaller range of people largely drawn from people who are paid to be in their lives, family and other people who are labeled disabled.

Given this reality people with disability labels have often been considered non-human throughout history. Even today some "experts" actively promote the notion that the personhood of people who are labeled disabled should be "measured", and, if they don't meet the standard, these "non-persons" should be permanently isolated in institutions or even killed. It could be natural to assume that lack of economic participation, responsibility and relationship are the inevitable outcomes of having clear physical, cognitive or emotional limitations. It could make sense to believe that all this adds up to diminished or nonexistent personhood. Why not believe that disability is a tragedy that must be accepted and coped with and that these limiting circumstances deprive a person of their essential identity? The evidence points to this!

There is a cultural shift in play, however. This change in beliefs declares that difference is not a tragedy but rather something to be understood and celebrated. The cultural shift I am referring to is the growing awareness that all human beings are persons by virtue of being born.

One benchmark of this new understanding was the proclamation of the United Nations Charter of Human Rights in 1949.

With this change in the way we value people has come an alteration in how we perceive limitations in people's minds and bodies. More often today we recognize that people who are labeled disabled are people with the same rights and possibilities as anyone else.

Once the truth that everyone is a person is accepted it becomes possible to see that society has placed many barriers in the way of people with unusual differences. These barriers destroy relationship, prevent contribution, and diminish capacity. The isolation, non-participation and lack of responsibility that seem to be caused by disability are in fact the result of the lack of appropriate support.

What is appropriate support? Citizens everywhere require the same sorts of support in order to take their places in society - transportation, housing, stable minimum income, education, information, relationship nurturing, etc. Different people need these supports in different ways. People with unusual bodies, minds and emotions need the same supports delivered in different ways, too!

Person Centred Planning is playing a significant part in shifting negative ideas about people with differences that get labeled "disability". Person Centred Planning is a set of powerful tools for discovering what roles a person can play and what contributions he or she can make. Person Centred Planning gives us a way to design and establish the citizenship supports a person needs so that places for them to play roles in the community can be revealed and sustained.Person Centred Planning has three great strengths. First every method of Person Centred Planning has a way for us to discover the unique strengths and gifts of the person at the center of the plan. Disability labels and environments often make it difficult to see a person's current contributions and how these contributions might fit into the community. For example a fascination with cars might be viewed as a behaviour problem if someone is living in a group home on a busy street. The same interest in cars is a requirement for working at the auto body shop in the same neighbourhood. Planning with a person in a personal way gives us a way to find the context that will give them opportunities to be respected and responsible.

Secondly, Person Centred Planning reveals the value of planning. To plan is to believe that the future is not already given - not fixed by physical and cognitive limitations or other circumstances. We are becoming more willing to say that something new can come into being for someone, then go about finding the people and resources to make it so. We are discovering that planning alternative futures is better not just for the individuals themselves but also for the various communities that they may come to participate in.

One young man I know has no eyes and is very vulnerable in his health. Throughout his high school years he has had a close group of friends who go to theme parks with him, create weekly musical gatherings at his house and regularly challenge his school environment to make a bigger space for him in their bureaucracy. For some months now they have been giving presentations at local schools about all they have gained from their many shared activities as a close band of friends. Their story also has been featured in their local community newspaper. Many, many people have been moved and enlightened by these young folks - their words and antics, their caring for each other and their spirit.

The planning that people do with this young man in order to create and sustain his public life is ongoing and creative. The results are not only beneficial for him but bring great value to his high school peers and to all the people of his town.

Thirdly, with Person Centred Planning comes the recognition that our efforts must not be focused first and foremost on caregivers and providers - as important as these people are. We are learning to take direction from the individual made vulnerable by being physically or functionally different.

Formerly, and - all too frequently still - planning comes down to little more than resource allocation. For example a service agency near where I live inherited a small warehouse eighteen months ago. From that day to this the agency's planning has focused on developing programs to carry out in this building. All the people served by this agency will be taking these programs whether the programs" objectives make sense in their lives or not!

Person Centred Planning makes us realize that the individual themselves can state the direction of their own life. Rather than assign prearranged lives to individuals, or turn only to caregivers to make decisions, we now have the means to turn on everyone's creative potential. For example, one young man dreamed of being a doctor. Rather than focusing on his lack of academic ability, the friends, family and service providers on his planning team carefully examined what it was about being a doctor that appealed to him. Now he has an important paying job at a hospital packing and distributing sterile surgical supplies. He is a respected member of his community.

Person Centred Planning gives us the flexibility to discover the right places for a person to be in and contribute to. It also opens up the invitation and opportunity for people to relate to the central person in ways that are more fulfilling and bring new resources, places and people into the picture.

For example, one middle-aged man is living in his own

apartment. He loves music and riding around in his car. His friends and personal assistants discovered that there were many small businesses in his neighbourhood where cars are repaired. Each one requires the daily services of a courier who picks up car parts from warehouses and delivers them to the garage. This man now has an independent business of his own, delivering car parts on short notice, working just as much as he wants to, and enjoying riding around in his own car.

Before having the opportunity to have a personal approach to planning his life, this man was served in a group home and an adult day care center. He was isolated and expensive to serve. Now, for a little less money than traditional services require, he contributes to the community, and is a member of a housing cooperative and an informal ring of independent couriers and mechanics. His supporters are backed up by a large network of interested and understanding neighbours and colleagues. Clearly he and his community are much further ahead.

Person Centred Planning is one aspect of an important cultural change. This change is one of recognizing the value of diversity in every aspect of life and relationship. This new perception focuses on the value of each individual and the importance of each person's unique contribution to the broader economy and community. Person Centred Planning is not just a new fad in support service tools of the trade, Instead Person Centred Planning is part of a bigger desire to build a world that works for all its citizens.

The Powell River Conversation. Part Three:
Building a Fire -"It is always all about the relationships"

*Julia Downs, Maria Glaze,
Aaron Johannes, Norman Kunc,
David Pitonyak, Shelley Nessman,
Jim Reynolds, Susan Stanfield,
Alison Taplay, Emma Van der Klift*

Maria: I had heard about Judith Snow at the Family Support Institute, but I had never heard her talk. I was very involved in the Provincial political will to have the system look different than it currently did. I was on committees and councils, but finally I had to back away from some of the stuff I was doing, because it was just depleting me. I was feeling really frustrated by it.

Well, then I heard Judith Snow talk at Naramata about all the systems advocacy she has done over the years, and about how she thinks systems are only really good at keeping people busy. Her advice was to just do what you want anyway, regardless of the systems that are in place. This helped me a lot, because I had basically given up on the idea of system change as a way to provide hope that my daughter will have a good life. What has worked for us is to just doing it anyway and finding a way to do that. That is what works for us. It was controversial at the training weekend, because a lot of families have invested a lot of time on these various councils and committees. For them, there was the worry that in giving up on systems our voices might not be heard. For me, the only thing that makes sense is to do what you think is right. Do it anyway. That was a powerful message for me.

Susan: It is true, Maria, isn't it? We could spend all our time at meetings and being on committees and focus groups and what have you. I personally have a natural resistance to that stuff, I find it pretty tedious. But I am also grateful that there are people out there who like doing that, because then I don't always have to. A lot of the machinery of it becomes the vogue, doesn't it? And we just keep doing what we are doing just to get to the same place or slightly beyond there, but we just keep living it and doing it.

Norman: The real revelation for us, I think, happened when we worked in New Mexico. New Mexico, several years ago, was about 48th in the nation around inclusion in schools. They got something like a 5 million dollar grant over five years. They brought in several people along with Emma and I every year for five years. There was one principal in particular who was doing some wonderful work.

He was the principal of an elementary school in one of the roughest neighbourhoods in Albuquerque. There were kids whose families were living in cars, there were gang issues, drive-by shootings, a really, really, rough school. The principal was enthusiastic and ready to implement a list of changes as long as your arm to make things better for the kids with disabilities in his school. In addition to embracing all of our recommendations, he decided he was going to shut down all their resource and time out rooms and deal with any problems with right there in the classroom. There was resistance from some of the staff, but most of them said, "Okay, I guess so." A wonderful special education prof down there named Liz Keefe helped them a lot. Eventually, it was suggested to the teachers and staff who wouldn't get on board that they transfer to another school.

By the end of the five years, that school was a model of inclusion in the States. The sense of community there was phenomenal. We'd show up and the kids would shout out "Hi, welcome to John Adams! Let me hold the door." However, that principal knew he was retiring in two or three years, and so he worked hard to create this incredible transition plan. He knew in advance who was going to be taking over, and had already cleared it with the school board. The staffing was all set up. Then the new principal came in. He stayed for a while, but the school district changed and he moved to a higher position. Someone else came in, and now that school has gone right back to being the most segregated school in Albuquerque. The fact is that even when you get it right, and even when you have a thoughtful person trying to figure out how to put all the sustainable pieces in place, the bureaucracy finds a way to put us back to where we were. It is like a one cell amoeba – it will always find a way to take care of its own survival. So that's always the second question: how do we maintain this wonderful new system? Because if you are not watching literally every second you are going to slide back, because systems always go the path of least resistance.

Emma: It is always all about the people. And that is why your boards and committees are so freaked out about you guys leaving. Because it is only ever about those relationships, that synergy between people, and the vision they hold together. We used to talk about this in Port Alberni. We'd say, "We want to make it so that everything we've worked so hard to create is safe and will continue in our absence (just in case we're hit by a bus)." But, of course, I now realize that it doesn't work that way.

David: I like to refer to that as the 'addiction to the boat.' Imagine there's a lake in front of you and there's a boat on the shore and your goal is to get across the lake. As a strategy, the boat makes a lot of sense. So you get in the boat and you go across the lake. The problem with our profession is that we get addicted to the boat. When we land on the other side of whatever it is, we still think we need the boat and, with much determination, carry it overland. We get addicted to the process – functional assessments, person-centered plans, risk assessment, whatever it might be - and we don't realize that we've gotten to the other side and now it's about our relationships.

Alison, this thing about being in a private place that is shared with a few and maybe there are some things about yourself that are just yours, I don't think the boat can make it happen. It is so dependent on the quality of our relationships. They may deepen because the boat was helpful along the way, but it's about a lot more than the boat.

Susan: Considering that idea of changing the system from within, I think there is still a part of us, as service providers, that believes it is possible, because that is what we are actively doing. The way I conceptualize it is that the traditional structure is like a pyramid. There's an agency with a board of directors at the top and the people at the bottom are the frontline staff and the people they're supporting; the recipients of all our hard work. I've got this graphic I show at our new staff orientations about taking that pyramid and flattening it out, so that the apex is the person and they have the weight of our whole organization behind them. It is kind of like that cell phone commercial for one of those networks where the guy is talking on his phone and the camera turns and we see about a million people behind him. He says, "This is my network." Well, we think that everyone out there who is affiliated with our organization – and I talk to new staff about this – whether it is Aaron or anyone who uses our services, that they all have the weight of our entire agency behind them. It's kind of an ah-ha moment for new staff when they think of their job in that way, instead of thinking of it as a hierarchy where they are down at the bottom with the people being supported. Because, after all, that is how most organizations work. The challenge for us is that this is also how our organization is structured; we do have a traditional structure with the board of directors, etcetera.

It is always interesting to me, in talking to people like you who see agencies from all over the world, that they are grappling with all of these same issues. I've talked to parents from all over who will say, " Well, isn't the ultimate goal that people won't need service providers, because communities will be so all-inclusive that everyone's needs will be met?" I know you, David, and Michael Kendrick have both tried to caution us, because that's not the goal: there will always need to be service providers. It is easy to dream of a Pollyanna-ish vision of a community that does everything for everybody and people not needing support. What we need to ask ourselves is how can we provide services in a way that empowers people and shifts the balance of power away from the agencies? I am curious, David, what do you think of that?

David: It seems to me that the question about changing the system from within is really about creating a community as an organization and leaving the system behind. That system is going to exist. It is not going to disappear anytime soon, but we can create an organization intentional to community and do our best to keep all that nonsense from the system from distracting us from what our true work is. There is just a way in which I think, in all likelihood, for at least some time to come, people are going to need our support and some of our abilities to organize things. If you're a family, for instance, who is exhausted and your back is against the wall, and people can come along who can help you to sort through some things and get organized around some things, I think that is an enormously helpful thing.

We can, for example, make it possible so that Moms and Dads can just be Moms and Dads, without having to be advocates and researchers and therapists and everything else. If we could, at least, let parents keep the hat they are most suited to wear – not that they don't want to be involved with any of this other stuff – and let them know that we can help with the things they want help with from time to time. That makes a lot of sense to me. And I think this kind of help will be needed for at least the foreseeable future.

But the piece that keeps coming back to me is this feeling like, if we could just get the Ministry, or whoever is in charge, to change their minds about things, it will take care of all of our stuff. To me, that looks to me like the kind of activity that makes us feel busy, but it is questionable over time whether it has any utility at all. The idea that people who are trying to manage a limited number of resources from a distance – that those people are going to have any idea at all what's going on – sounds preposterous to begin with. Maybe sometimes they can deal with a part of it, but a lot of times all they are doing is slowing us down from what we are doing that really does make a difference, which is spending time getting to know people and figuring out what works for them as individuals. This is so much more organic. I think there is a way to figure out how to do that. I think there is a way to be sane about that.

Our friend in Vermont, Al Vecchione of the Francis Foundation, says it comes up all the time. We are busy with all this stuff, interfacing with the system. But we know in our heart of hearts that what makes a real difference in the future prospects of people's lives and in the quality of their lives is who shows up and spends time with them. It was true 100 years ago. It is true now. It will be true 100 years from now. Whatever the technology, whatever the drugs, this personal connection is still going to be absolutely critical to success. It is tried and true.

But we also know that if we don't respond to the system it hammers us, it wears us down. So what we do is we get organized about what the system needs, but we don't take it too seriously. It's almost as if professionals feel that they are children in desperate need of approval ...Hopefully, we will wake up one day and realize we already *are* adults. We don't need to wait around for Mom and Dad's approval. And then we finally realize we are adults and we are no longer waiting around for Mom and Dad to define what is okay and not okay. We don't care if the system is not going to hold a parade for us anytime soon. We do know what makes a difference in people's lives. It's not all that confusing. Our problem, historically, has always been staying focused on this and not getting distracted by the fifteen or sixteen things the system needs.

To me, it looks like we are still kind of hoping that somehow we are all going to collaborate and that it is all going to get easier. And I think, first of all, those people at that system level are in an impossible position to make heads or tails about what is going on in my life, or your life, in anyone's life, except maybe the people closest to them.

Norman: There is another piece to add to that. I am thinking of Tom Skrtic. He's a prof at the University of Kansas who is really involved in inclusive education and writes a lot about it. His concern is with the bureaucratization of schools. He says that one of the problems that arise from the bureaucratization of education – and this equally true of the human service field – is that it is a function of bureaucracy to minimize discretion. The less discretion people have in their work, the more uniformity you can create. You are then able to reliably rein in your people in order to keep the whole system running efficiently. In this context, he talks about the mechanization of teaching. Unfortunately, over the last forty years school systems have tried and almost succeeded in removing discretion from teaching. Tom says, "Of course this is a problem, because teaching is all about discretion." In fact, that is the magic of teaching.

Part of the problem in trying to fix any system to more efficiently meet the needs of its constituents is that the system by definition needs regimentation. That is how it functions. And so we're trying to implement discretion in a system that thrives on regimentation. No wonder it doesn't work well!

The other thing Tom asks is what do you do when you have this large bureaucracy and you've got to get stuff done? His response is that, when that happens, a variety of groups have to come together within the school or within the organization. They might get together for beer, or at somebody's house, or in the staff room, and decide, okay, why don't we just do this; and then just go ahead and do it. He calls this change process 'adhocracy'. These are the networks of people that come together informally within a bureaucracy – and this is where the real work happens. Unfortunately, the problem that sometimes arises when you get an adhocracy going is that people then want to systematize it. What we fail to realize is that it works precisely because it is not systematized!

Emma: Norm and Malerie Meeker and I did some facilitation for a group of executive directors a couple of months back. We talked about getting bogged down in the needs of the system. My part of the discussion was about pushing the pause button and slowing things down in order to create space for reflection. In a world café discussion that I facilitated, Cam Dore said, "I know exactly how to slow the system down. Involve the people you support in all aspects of the process. For example, I never negotiate anything with the government without bringing somebody that I support with me. It automatically just slows the process down." This makes sense on every level.

Susan: Ernie, our executive director, is very involved at the Provincial level and spends a lot of time involved with those communities and working from within. And I think he has been very successful at it. He has made a big difference. He is respected by all sides: bureaucrats and government people, as well as those in need of services. It takes a lot of intentional work in order to build that respect. But we know small organizations doing great work who live in fear that at the stroke of a pen the latest commissioner, because they always keep changing, they will be wiped out of existence. There are all these little pockets of hope, but they are all so, so vulnerable, because they're exceptions; they are tiny fish in a big sea. They could easily be wiped out.

Aaron: One of the things I really admire about most of these little agencies is that they are all very predictive about what the system wants, and I think we have also figured out how to do that. We know what our government, at its best, is trying to do and we know that they don't always have that capacity or the skills to really do it. So, we will create it for them and write it up, and we are not insistent about taking the credit for it – it's not about getting the credit. And what we hope is that this grows more potential and more possibility. And things shift, just a little forward movement ...

David: But being in those roles that they are taking at government and large funding agencies and allowing other people to write the book or the script is not a small act of courage, either. Sure, sometimes there is a kind of complicity to it – a way in which we are giving them information about things that are working well and they are feeding it back to others, but they are also running a lot of risk in the fact that they'll, in a way, give it cover for a while, so that you can get it done. This is no small deal.

Maria: I'm not sure if this is relevant, so stop me if I am off track here. I am thinking of good organizations and what I miss about them. We have a microboard for our daughter and our microboard is spread out geographically, so they are not as involved in our lives or as closely connected as I think other microboards might be. We have two acres with two houses and Rebecca goes back and forth between the houses. I hire all the staff and we have those relationships that happen. I have been thinking about this kind of like, when I go to the doctor, I know my body, so I want a doctor who says, tell me what you think is going on. And then, with that information in mind, he can tell me what he thinks will help.

I don't have the time or the energy to research and make critical choices about every medication. I want to find somebody I trust who will do that work for me, and I can go to them and say, okay, what ideas do you have? I feel the same way in terms of Rebecca's support and her microboard. I don't want, anymore, to go to every conference out there, being solely responsible to be the collector of information. And it doesn't necessarily make sense to just send one staff person to all this, either. So, I miss having an organization around. I miss having people around who I could discuss ideas with, people who have been out there reaping all these great ideas that I could potentially have access to, people who could support us. I could say I know Rebecca very well, and collectively all of us on her microboard, in our various ways, can provide an overall wisdom of what we know about Rebecca. But it would be nice to have other people who could do some of that leg-work and bring new information and energy back to us.

I want to be a Mom who misses her kid and wants to have her over for dinner. I don't want to be the supervisor of the staff. I don't want to do all the information gathering, so I love knowing that there are organizations who are doing some of that fundamental work with people who might come into our lives, or who could make me aware of what's new, or who know where the effective connections are for the people who do the amazing support they do with my daughter and where they can go to be around people who are talking about that stuff that energizes them. Because we often feel alone. So, I hope these organizations never go away, because I really so appreciate and I am so grateful that you are out in the world thinking about, and working on, and doing these things, and can bring it back and support families like mine, because the only other option for us is to go and be taken over by a big agency.

Aaron: In terms of an agency, its role might be what you were talking about, Emma, where the job at the end is making sure that all those connections come together, and that we are expanding those connections. It's a learning group. You start with some connections and then grow those connections. This TASH committee I am on, it is the same kind of thing. It has an agenda, but the usefulness for me is more about the relationships that have developed.

I think what is interesting is trying to imagine what people who are coming into this field might do instead of the kinds of job descriptions we give them. If we say to them, your job is now networking, then how does that work? And I know that we keep meeting people who are really good networkers from all around the Province, and they come to our workshops and they say, "I should tell you, I get the worst evaluations of anyone in my whole agency. Because I am really bad at paperwork and I am the worst housekeeper ever, and I keep taking people to parties instead of doing all that other stuff. But I just really love those people and we have such a good time." It is this sort of outlaw role.

And I don't know if the way to teach people about how to do it is to legitimize the role, or if it is really about continuing conversation and reflection opportunities. One of our friends who has done a lot of this work says, "I don't understand why people keep needing to hear this. I was there 11 years ago and I taught this class – how come they don't remember?" And the fact is, a lot of them have changed jobs, and even the ones who were there 11 years ago probably forgot what you were talking about, and in between these talks there have been a lot of other things that they are told to pay attention to. And so I wonder if it is just about continuing the conversation.

David: Something I've been going through, just energetically, in my work lately (and I have been flashing to this image several times during our conversation) is that there's a part of me that just wants to build a fire. I find myself just wanting to go and build a fire down by the water. I want to be the guy collecting the wood and getting the fire started. I hope it doesn't seem like I don't want to talk today – I find our conversation invigorating and really wonderful. But this conversation happens to be occurring at a time in my life when, more and more, I feel like doing things like building a fire and really not doing much at all, frankly. You know, there is just something about that image for me right now in my life that is important to me and I'm not even entirely sure of all of what it is. But I also think that there is a way in which the person doing the community building, those people who may work for an agency where everything is needed in a rush, paperwork and such, but who still are real community builders – I think they get, that on some level, it is about doing and not so much about hurrying to do. These connectors know that it is about being in a time frame with people, the need to go from being in a hurry and too busy, to being present and consistent. When you think about status and the social brain, we live longer with status. We live longer when we are valued by the pack.

So, in organizations that really value the community builder, the person who is helping others to make these leaps – they understand the time frames and the pace of it all, but they truly understand the value of community. I think that an understanding of the importance of community builders is often part of what is missing.

I find sometimes that I am so far from the fire that it is unbelievable. Part of me, just in my own brain, is telling me that I just need a time out here. I just have to get down and do nothing for a while around that fire, even just to see if this is all making any sense, or whether I am just having trouble keeping up right now.

All the things that annoy us about community builders when we are managers working in systems; this stuff is, in reality, the essential work. It is natural, and a lot of the other stuff we do is unnatural. We spend too much time taking these natural processes and trying to turn them into part of the machinery of a system, and I don't think this can work. So, I get worried about us when we just add more layers. Like you were saying, Norm, technology could potentially become a bunch of information that is potentially helpful, but it also, if it is used as a replacement for true connection, could be the kind of stuff that further adds to our feelings of being overwhelmed. It might have been good, in the first place, to just go and sit down by the fire. I like the idea of just talking to people as an alternative to reading a lot of stuff. Although, having said all that, these *Ted Talks* and such – these seem really interesting to me.

Emma: Much of what Norm and I get sent from colleagues and friends these days shows up in the form of a poem or a short video that someone loved, something on youtube, etc. Not only do people not have time to read lengthy treatises, there seems to be a real hunger for a different kind of dialogue. And, you're right, David, the conversations we have are very nourishing. Even though we may not always have the luxury of having them face to face, they *can be* in person in a different way. As a society, we're reinventing how dialogue happens. The conversation has the potential to become broader and more inclusive regardless of geography.

Maria: What I have always valued is that I can read something and I can watch something, but what energizes me most is when I can sit with someone like Shelley and have a deep and emotional conversation about it. A kind of mushrooming happens because of the energy we have together – energy that I don't get from reading alone. Because I can sit and stew about it, but I don't get the benefit of where she may go with that information. For example, the person who supports my daughter in the community – when we want to look at doing things more deeply entrenched in this kind of (person-centred) work, it reminds me of the idea that if we have someone clapping a new rhythm, but everyone else keeps clapping the old rhythm – pretty soon we just get back to clapping that same old rhythm. We have people who are trying to play with new ideas – perhaps they have just come from a great workshop and they are all pumped up – but they go back to their day-to-day lives and little by little they stop being energized by that. So, if someone has some new ideas, they need to have a network they can go to and talk about them and keep them alive and growing. We need the network to support them and to be energized by them. It is disheartening for supporters to take new information back to a place where they know people are going to keep doing the same old things regardless.

Shelley: Maria and I took drumming lessons. A world-renowned percussionist was teaching five of us. He taught us all a pattern, and then he taught us how to start doing our own individual pattern. At first we sounded horrible and it was hard for us not to play what each other were playing. But in the end, after a period of time, it was amazing what we produced, all doing something a little bit different. We learned how to work together doing our different thing. I've been thinking more and more about dialogue – how to talk to and hear and listen to folks. There are two ideas really coming together for me right now. And these are 1) the importance of dialogue and 2) how we can take *everywhere* this lesson we've learned today about the importance of open ended conversations, and use it wherever we are.

In my new job I am astounded at the richness of the conversations I am having with everybody, because people are just walking up to me and sharing these amazingly deep and thoughtful ideas. It has been so enriching and it has taken me to a million new places. I have been in a number of different jobs in this field and this depth of conversation is not the case everywhere, so I just want to grow these opportunities out, so that it becomes the culture wherever we are. I love what Alison said about the challenges of the family being the opportunity or the *gift* of community, and the idea that we should grow these opportunities and encourage these gifts until community is fully embedded. Because talking about things is the first step in getting things done, making things happen.

Susan: This conversation has really helped reinforce what I have been writing about. It reinforces, also, how timely it is and how important that we get together and share this information. Our field has been convinced over and over again that it has had the right idea at the right time. We have often heard people saying *"Now* we have got the right way of doing things." I talk about not being too over-confident or overzealous about any new method, no matter how good it seems, and so, resisting putting labels on things and calling this a new method or a new approach. But to me now, it feels like we are turning to a hundred years ago – to things that would have made sense to our grandparents – getting together in community and helping each other. A lot of the nonsense that has happened in the years since has probably left our ancestors wondering what the heck we were doing. It feels like we are returning now to a place of simplicity, of common sense and humanity, and undoing a lot of the *stuff* that has failed people in the past.

David: And I guess, in some ways, this has helped me to get started building that fire I was talking about.

Norman: In all of the conferences I have been to, all the workshops, all the AGM's, and all the training, no one ever had a session where they said, "Limited to eight people, let's just get together and talk." And what struck me today is where this conversation went. It started off with all of us thinking about information. You know, what can we do, what do we need to know? Even David's idea around being tired of having to endlessly research stuff and learn about new stuff. What has been fascinating for me is that we started off thinking we need information, but what we realized is that what we really need are people. In a way we started off looking in the wrong place. It's like that old joke about the man who is looking for his wallet under a streetlight at night. A policeman comes up to him and asks him where he last had his wallet and he says he doesn't know. So the policeman asks why he's looking under the streetlight if he didn't lose his wallet there. He replies "because the light is better here". We start off looking for information, maybe because the light is better – in other words, it is easier and more concrete to do this – but what we really need is to look somewhere else – to build connections. I think we just keep looking in the wrong place.

Emma: I guess, because Norm and I have been so very involved for the last two or three years in learning about narrative approaches and narrative therapy, I have been thinking about this from a narrative perspective. In a narrative view, the goal is to have different conversations than we've ever had before. And this is accomplished through genuine curiousity and by taking a larger view. One of the things we talk about in the narrative community is that unfortunately, most of us tend to privilege our problem saturated stories and tell them to ourselves and each other over and over again. This isn't to minimize the challenges, but we need to be aware that by privileging these stories we simultaneously push the alternative stories to the margins. What a narrative therapist will do when a client is stuck in a problem saturated story is to listen very carefully for the exceptions – times when that story wasn't defining everything. Those exceptions are always, always present. I was hearing a lot of that here today. There are problems, but there are other times when amazing things happen, and that's what you build on. But you don't build by cheerleading and pushing people, by saying, "Look at you – you did so do this wonderful thing!" No. It is more about asking genuinely curious questions about the nature of those exceptions, how they came to be, and what meaning people make of them. It's about digging deeper, thickening the story, if you will. I felt like we were doing a lot of that today, and I really value that. Michael White, one of the first people to start the narrative therapy movement, called these exceptions "sparkling moments". We have to be intentional in noticing them, because they are often fleeting and easy to lose in the chaos of daily life. But *that* is where we have to go, because that's where the gold is. I feel like we have done some of that today.

Aaron: I was reading this thing last night by Peter Park, one of the founders of People First in Canada. He was in an institution for 18 years. He refers to himself as 33 years old, even though he is really 51, because those years in the institution didn't really exist for him. He is an incredibly brilliant guy. He was talking about self-determination and he said, "You know, I have been kicked out of meetings where I have tried to put this on the agenda, and I just really enjoy the opportunity to bring these issues more to the forefront. I look at it like it is a challenge just to get self-determination on the agenda." That is his happiness. He said, "I don't think it is that high on the agenda yet, but at least it's there. And we've got some friends, and so that's a step in the right direction. It might be small right now, but we get more powerful as time goes on. People take time to change; it doesn't come in a hurry. Real change always comes slowly. But, change that doesn't mean change always comes in a heck of a hurry." When Susan was talking about this whole idea of returning to simplicity and humanness, these kinds of values, the thing that keeps coming up for me are that people like Barb Goode and Peter Park and others we know who bring that richness to communities that are hungry for what we actually know how to do – that together we know more about than anybody else. It seems to me, increasingly, like it is truly a gift to be involved in this field. We are meeting with people who are doing this work and have been doing it for years, as well as people who are just starting and want to find a hopeful place to come into it. When I watch the actual interactions we are having, it is incredibly hopeful and inspiring. I think, yeah, I could do this all over again.

Jim: So much hits me all at once – the idea of insisting on honesty, and about having more open ended conversations like this one, on slowing down and making sure we are doing things right. I hope that conversations like this will spread and grow.

Norman: Those are some good final points, Jim. One thing that kept coming up in Emma's research on hostage negotiation is how important it is to slow things down. Emma was talking about this with her research supervisor, Alfie Kohn, and he said, "That reminds me of a bumper sticker I saw that said, *don't just do something, stand there.*" think this is the beauty of what we have done here today. Because a lot of people could look at this and say, "But there was no agenda. You didn't come up with any action plan." The beauty of what we did here today was that we didn't just do something, we stood here.

Maggie's Contributions
Erin Sheldon

When my daughter Maggie was four years old, she almost died. It was Labour Day weekend. We'd spent the summer preparing for Maggie to start Junior Kindergarten, so that long holiday weekend started out full of anticipation and worry. Would she transition well? Would she enjoy it? Had we prepared everything she needed? Would she receive enough support? Would everyone be kind? Then Maggie went into respiratory failure and spent the next three weeks on a ventilator. She started kindergarten long after her classmates did, frail and weak from what we came to call her Big Illness.

The Big Illness was a turning point for us, as Maggie's parents. Until that illness, when I thought of Maggie being included with her typically developing classmates, I worried that Maggie would need too much support and be unable to participate. I worried she wouldn't make friends or would not be liked. In the back of my mind, I believed that including Maggie was doing her a favour because she requires more resources and assistance than her classmates. I hoped no one begrudged her the extra resources she consumed just by being there. To me, including Maggie was an act of benevolence. Before that illness, I hoped that Maggie would learn from her classmates' good example and that they would be kind to her in return.

After the Big Illness, everything changed. Afterwards, I understood that Maggie is a survivor. I witnessed her fight her way back to good health. I witnessed her endure the after-effects of muscle-wasting and drug withdrawal from ICU medications. I witnessed her push her body as hard as she could to regain strength and to finally be able to walk again. I witnessed as she developed migraines as an aftereffect of the intubation. I watched her learn she could express that a migraine was coming and to seek help coping with the pain. Suddenly, I realized that Maggie was a role model for everyone in her classroom community. No one was doing her any favours by including her. Instead, they were fortunate to have her as part of them.

I now understand that Maggie is a powerful role model on many levels. In her kindergarten class, she modeled resilience and cheerfulness in the face of challenges and even suffering. Every day, she set herself the task of enjoying the day, whatever it might bring, and pushing her own body to allow her to do the most she could do. I began to wish that more adults had role-models like Maggie when we were children. Above all, Maggie's Big Illness made me realize that her time on this earth is valuable and must not be wasted.

As my own thinking changed, I realized that much of the rest of the world had not changed with us. The professionals in Maggie's life seemed to see a child who was even needier than the one before the Big Illness. She received a new label: "medically fragile." Physicians saw disease and helplessness where I saw a survivor. Her therapists saw a broken body that needed remediation and discipline, rather than respect for what her body had endured and how hard that body worked. I watched school professionals set goals for Maggie's learning that were based on an image of her as a helpless toddler; they looked to the toddler norm for what she needed to learn at school as though the goal was that she achieve all the toddler skills so she could move on to achieving preschool skills, with little regard for her chronological age. They seemed to see her as their neediest student but I saw Maggie as their teacher.

I came to understand that I cannot just be Maggie's mother. I am also her witness. Part of my duty as Maggie's witness is to testify to what I observe in my girl. I have come to believe that the biggest impact of Maggie's disabilities on her individual freedom is that she is vulnerable to having other people tell her story for her. Worse, some people seem to assume that she has no story to tell at all. Maggie's medical labels, developmental assessments, personal support plan and Individual Education Plan tell one kind of story about her. That story often focuses on her failures to achieve a kind of mythical norm of what a child is supposed to do by certain times in the lifespan; the explanation for her differences is found in the failures of her body and brain. I choose to tell a new story that challenges this professional explanation of Maggie's differences. To me, Maggie's story is one of opportunity, resilience and hard work.

Maggie offers opportunity in abundance: to experience deep human connection, learning, and contribution. The test for the rest of us is whether we choose to receive what she offers or if we fail to even notice it's there. She is only 8, and yet she has learned more about persistence and hard work than any child I know. She harnesses the effort of an unruly body every day without appearing to blame that body for making her any different. Her buoyant good spirits are the definition of resilience.

One of the contributions Maggie makes to those around her is that she is authentic. This is particularly important at her current age of 8. I watch how girls learn to act cool, often by adopting new behaviours and codes that separate the "cool girls" from the not-cool. I witness how girls this age respond to the pressure to grow up before their time by trying to be mini-adults. It breaks my heart that they seem to equate "mature" behaviour with sarcasm and clique-formation. It begs the question of how can we stop sending our girls the message that nastiness and exclusion are part of mature adulthood? Maggie is authentic in the face of this pressure to be cool or artificial. She responds with casual authenticity to the behaviours of the girls around her; she is not easily impressed but she is easily amused, and she laughs at their silliness in a way that gently exposes the pretense. She ignores the signals from other girls about whether a certain child has been deemed cool versus unworthy. This is a gift that Maggie offers to all the girls she knows. For the girls who are trying desperately to act cool, Maggie's authenticity tells them it's OK, they don't need to be anyone other than themselves for her to like them. Similarly, for the girls who have been left out or excluded from the cool cliques, Maggie communicates to them that it's OK, they don't need to change to be liked. I witness Maggie creating a safe space where it's OK to just be you.

Maggie appears to be equally accepting of herself. I'm not sure I've ever seen someone with such easy self-confidence. I have witnessed her body fail to do what she needs it to do, and I've only ever seen her try harder. I've never felt she was blaming herself for what her body can't do or even blaming her own body. She appears to accept her body and its limitations. She delights in its abilities and maximizes all of them. She is a strong role-model for healthy self-esteem.

Maggie is just as authentic as a student in her classroom. I've witnessed how classrooms seem to cast each student into a certain role: we know which student is the smart one, the good one, the bad one, and so on. I see how a classroom community can accept these roles and perpetuate them, constantly interpreting each student's behaviour within the confines of the role they have been cast in. I have seen the pressure this puts on each student: if you are the smart one, then you must always have the answers. If you are the good one, then you must never misbehave. If you are the bad one, then you must go to extraordinary lengths to be seen as good when it's often easier to just give people the "bad" they seem to expect. Maggie does not subscribe to these roles. She engages with each student based on how they are with her, not with how she is "supposed" to interpret them. She sends a message that every student is smart when they are with her. She allows the "good girls" to relax their guard and be silly, and creates space for the "bad" kids to be smart, competent and helpful. In this way, Maggie challenges the restrictions of classroom roles and creates space to imagine richer understandings of each student.

Maggie teaches other people to trust non-verbal communication. She does not speak with words. Maggie expresses herself with her eyes, her hands, her face, the tone of her voice and her entire body. She is a fluent communicator. Her face and her vocalizations leave little doubt about how she feels. She encourages people to trust what someone's body is telling you rather than what their words say. Maggie exposes the failures of spoken language by ignoring words when a person's eyes and body tell a different story. She does not accept our society's polite, tacit agreement to let verbal communication trump the non-verbal; if someone says they are fine when they are clearly not, she will wait in silence to hear what is not being said.

Maggie is deeply honest. She is not restrained by politeness. She often expresses what everyone is feeling but is too polite to say. If a classroom lecture is boring or a car ride is long and uncomfortable, Maggie expresses with her body and her voice what everyone else likely wants to say, too. If Maggie had words, I cannot imagine she would ever respond to "how are you?" with "fine, thank you." I think that because she has no words, she doesn't rely on trite phrases. Maggie exposes the ways in which our motivation to be polite and appropriate prevents us from speaking with genuine honesty or sharing our struggles with others. The polite shorthand of "I'm fine, thank you" leaves little room for us to connect with other people. Our local community has been rocked by the tragedy of university students disguising their depression until the disease results in suicide; to me, this is the ultimate expression of everything that is wrong with a world where we have learned phrases like "I'm fine" to disguise our true feelings, and worse, where we have learned to accept those phrases at face value. Maggie teaches us about the importance of honestly expressing our emotions to others so that we can then feel human connection.

Maggie is forgiving in how she interprets the actions of others. I see her when a classmate misbehaves, yells, or flings out their arms. I see her when her best friend is mean. Maggie seems to accept these behaviours with curiosity about what might come next, rather than with hurt. She might walk away from the friend or classmate if their behaviour stops being interesting, but she doesn't appear to take their actions personally. In contrast, I see other children focus on their own hurt feelings in the same situations, such that they can't see past their own hurt to listen to what the hurtful child may have been communicating. Maggie, however, appears willing to sit back and wait for friends to return to their usual selves. Better yet, she is often willing to wait with them: gently accepting, quietly curious, self-entertaining, present but not pushy. In this forgiving approach, I witness Maggie appearing to suspend her own ego in her interpretation of other people's actions.

Maggie is uninhibited in the way she expresses her curiosity in other people. Norman Kunc encourages us to "seek the story in the stranger"; Maggie does this every day, everywhere she goes. She seeks the story with her eye contact, expressing interest in most people she sees. She seeks the story with her curiosity in their handbags and the contents of their shopping carts. She wants to see the inside of their vehicles and their homes. She particularly appreciates the convenience of camera rolls on iPhones and other smart phones; Maggie loves to take someone's iPhone and won't voluntarily give it back until she has seen every picture on their device. There is no one else I know who is willing to sit with me and view every picture of my life experience! Through their pictures, Maggie explores her curiosity about the life and experiences of the people she meets. In a perfect Maggie world, everyone would carry an iPhone with a full camera roll and would exchange iPhones in lieu of greetings.

Maggie is a formidable community organizer. I often say that when I go to the grocery store without Maggie, I am just another anonymous housewife. But when I am with Maggie, she thrusts me into conversations with everyone we meet. You cannot be anonymous in Maggie's presence. She is remembered wherever she goes. Maggie exposes how, in our everyday lives, most of us avoid interaction with others. We use pay-at-the-pump and automated tellers to avoid interaction with cashiers. We politely avert eye contact in elevators and public washrooms. We don't talk to strangers. We don't comment on the groceries selected by the other people in line at the grocery store. Our polite reserve is perhaps our greatest barrier to having cohesive supportive community, for what kind of society would we be if we were never curious about each other? Maggie insists on interaction with most people she encounters. She creates connections and memories in ordinary, mundane moments we would never otherwise value or remember. I can't think of anyone who has had a passing conversation with me in the recent past who will smile if they ever remember the encounter, but I know that dozens of people do this every day when they think of Maggie.

Maggie models a delight in being young. She loves sensory play such as finger-painting with shaving cream or touching flowing water. I watch girls work so hard to portray themselves as older than their years, and I witness their palpable relief when they can just delight in being young. Recently, my 5 year old told me that she was sad I am a grown-up because "grown-ups are too busy to catch snowflakes on their tongues". I realized with shock that I need more of Maggie's influence to re-teach me the delight in being agelessly young. I've witnessed Maggie create space for countless people to experience the healing delight of just reveling in the simple sensations of flowing water or the comedy of gravity making things fall.

Maggie genuinely celebrates diversity and difference. I think her favourite thing in the whole world is to be surprised by the unexpected. She appears to live in a constant state of hopeful anticipation that the next moment will be less predictable than the last. Maggie is genuinely excited when a new person has unexpected differences. She has a particular appreciation for assistive equipment such as walkers, wheelchairs and oxygen tanks. Maggie thus role-models being comfortable with human diversity. I am not comfortable with difference the way Maggie is. Unexpected difference makes me anxious. Should I make eye contact with the panhandler? If I do, am I now obligated to give money? What response is appropriate when I'm confronted with a woman who appears catatonic on a stretcher? How should I talk to someone whose body is contorted by disability? Maggie role-models total comfort combined with curiosity and genuine appreciation for difference when confronted by these same encounters that provoke anxiety in me.

Maggie appears to reserve judgement on differences in other people. If anything, she privileges difference over the approximation of normality. My observation of Maggie is that she approaches other people with little expectation that they are supposed to be any certain way. She seems to notice but not judge differences in how people act, talk and move. Maggie appreciates unexpected movements and unpredictable sounds in the people she meets. Walking on a sidewalk in our little town, it is the panhandler who attracts her interest, precisely because she is so different from the other people walking briskly past. Maggie's attraction to difference has led her to gently stroke the stub of an amputated limb or a face sunken by disease and coated with drool. I've watched her approach a stretcher where a woman with a body contorted by disease could only moan and stare; Maggie crouched to put her face at the level of the woman's eyes, then giggled in delight at the human connection. I am profoundly humbled by these moments when it is Maggie alone who seems to always see the humanity where I can only see the suffering or difference. Maggie's acceptance of difference in the human body is something I struggle to emulate.

Maggie appears to accept that we all need help sometimes. She role-models how to request and receive assistance on her own terms. She does not appear to put any particular significance on her need for assistance; she seems to accept it as normal. If she needs help with her balance, she'll reach out for the nearest person and smile her appreciation as she grabs whatever body part was most convenient for her purposes. She doesn't ask for more assistance than she needs and she usually attempts a task before she asks for help. But Maggie is easily more accepting and aware of her own personal limits than any other person I know. She actively requests that others scaffold her to do the things she can't achieve on her own. Maggie does not appear to be self-conscious that she might be a burden to other people. Instead, she appears to act on a confident belief that she has the right to receive assistance, without placing any value or judgement on her need for it. I witness her create opportunities for other people to experience being helpful, and to thus receive her warm, casual appreciation. I notice that people need to be needed and they bloom when they feel they feel they made a difference; I see that Maggie helps them meet this need. Janet Klees refers to this as an act of grace, of Maggie bestowing a moment where she takes second place so that someone else can experience the act of giving.

Similarly, Maggie is confident in her right to decline assistance from others. Sometimes, she finds over-assistance amusing and she will hang, giggling, on the person who tries to do for her something that she can do herself. More often, though, she will shake off a helping hand that infringes on her personal space. She does not politely tolerate assistance she doesn't want. In this way, Maggie insists on the right to define her own needs and meet them as she sees fit. Maggie is thus an advocate for her right to self-determination. She is comfortable receiving support and confident defining the conditions under which support is helpful.

Maggie is forgiving, but she takes it personally when you limit her autonomy. She models non-violent passive resistance in the face of controlling authority. Gandhi would appreciate her direct action tactics. If adults ignore her when she tells is telling us how she feels about something, she will drop on the spot with quiet confidence in her right to control where her body goes. She won't get up until I've acknowledged what she's expressing, negotiated a compromise, and apologized for not listening. I've never felt that Maggie wants an apology from anyone but me, and I have to apologize to her all too often. Maggie keeps me honest by demonstrating that she trusts me to listen to her so that I can become aware of my errors, acknowledge them, and remedy them.

Maggie thus models how to be an active agent in her own life. I see her constantly expressing what she wants to do and learning to negotiate for her interests in the face of other people with different agendas. Maggie is not obedient for obedience's sake. She needs a reason to do what I ask, and I need to persuade her that what I want is worth her time and cooperation. Maggie is a powerful self-advocate. I see Maggie's young friends and the vulnerability created by their desires to be loved, liked and receive approval; I witness Maggie role-modeling a way of being loved and liked that doesn't hinge on obedience or approval.

Maggie demands excellence in teaching. She does not appreciate a classroom arranged with no regard to universal design for learning: she insists on intense interaction with her learning materials. Maggie wants to move, to see, to hear, to feel, and especially to touch. She insists that her classroom learning is personally relevant and that it adds something to her understanding of the world. She does not learn for her teacher's sake, she only learns for her own. Maggie's curiosity about that which is novel or unusual is easily harnessed for the sake of learning when teachers are imaginative and creative. Maggie disciplines teachers to use more visuals and real objects. She insists teachers create space for physical movement in learning. She models self-advocacy by showing how a student can exert influence on a teacher to meet her own learning needs. Through this process, she improves the learning for many other students who might be less effective in their advocacy or less passionate about receiving meaningful content in interesting ways.

The most profound contribution I find Maggie makes is that she is willing to expose herself to suffering. She demonstrates no fear that suffering is contagious. Maggie appears to feel no obligation to offer comfort or to try and make things better. She is able to be present without inserting her own ego into another person's experience of pain or grief. Her presence is a silent comfort that doesn't demand attention or reassurance. She is deeply comfortable with silence. There is no need to tell her it's OK, she can go, you'll be alright, because her authenticity and deep honesty express that she will leave when she feels ready -she is not present out of obligation. To me, Maggie's ability to be present with no strings attached is the definition of witnessing and solidarity.

Maggie is a gifted witness. Witnessing is often understood as a verb: the act of giving first-hand testimony to something that has transpired. But a deeper, older understanding of the noun, a "witness", is someone who is present without judgement or ego. When I worked closely with faith communities on issues of social justice, I heard spiritual leaders refer to how Jesus Christ asked his followers to "*be* witness." Later, when I prepared for the birth of my children, I was struck by medical literature showing that women in childbirth report less pain when they are in the presence of others, even if the other person stood silently behind a screen such that only his feet were visible to the labouring mother. As I witness my children grow, I am nourished by those moments of being fully present with them, without judgement, with only delight in all that is unique about them. In all these understandings of "witness", the act of giving testimony comes second to simply being present in a shared experience with acceptance rather than judgement. To witness means to make another person not alone without infringing on their own experience. Maggie is the consummate witness.

Maggie is witness to the world exactly as it is. I perceive Maggie as a deeply private girl who keeps her own counsel. Even if she was so inclined, Maggie's ability to provide testimony is an act that could be challenged in court. It is thus my role, as her mother, to witness Maggie in the world and give testimony to her contribution and the depth of her experience. Testimony from a witness is the evidence that our society uses to make judgement about guilt versus innocence, worth versus unworth. This, then, is my first-hand testimony of the contributions Maggie makes in the world.

Acknowledgements

On behalf of the press, first of all, we'd like to thank all the authors and interviewees and interviewers who contributed to this conversation, many volunteering their work and time. Thank you. We also appreciate the respective publishers and organizations who allowed us to reprint works which had appeared elsewhere. Given that Spectrum Press is a social enterprise it is in keeping with our practices that self advocates received a small honorarium, and we wish it could be more.

W. C. Gaventa's article, "Rekindling commitment: reflections from a pastoral educator enmeshed in direct support professional workforce development and person centered supports," was originally published in the *Journal of Intellectual Disability Research,* Volume 52, Part 7 (July 2008), and is reprinted here with permission under license 2957431444489.

Michael Kendrick's article, "What Remains Worth Struggling For," was originally published in *Relationships and Everyday Lives: People With A Disability and Vital Communities*, CRU Publications, Brisbane, Australia (2003) and is reprinted here with permission. CRU (Community Resource Unit) publications and projects may be viewed on their site at www.cru.org.au

David Pitonyak's "The Importance of belonging" first appeared in *Connections* (January/February 2006), the magazine of TASH, and is reprinted here with their permission. For more information about TASH and how to join, please visit www.tash.org

Judith Snow's article is hosted at www.capacitythinking.org.uk

Tim Stainton's "Empowerment and the architecture of rights based social policy," was originally published in Sage Publication's *Journal of Intellectual Disabilities* and is provided to this anthology with permission through License Number: 2964040417975

Both Paul Young and Peter Park's interviews with Patrick McDonagh were originally part of Patrick's project, "The Label Game," www.labelgame.org

As for me, I'd like to thank Patrick McDonagh and Jim Reynolds for their constant and gracious responsiveness to my questions and emails. I work with an amazing team of people – Ernie Baatz, Susan Stanfield, Shelley Nessman, Judy Wong (and of course, Jim) and Barb Goode, and a leadership team that supports this division of our organization by allowing us to focus on this "research and development" piece. Thanks for this!

Last, I'd like to thank my own family, who have such endless patience with these projects – Gary just came to ask if I was okay, as it's 4 a.m.! I am, indeed, partly exhilarated and partly very aware of a deadline! Thanks to him, and to Zev and Amanda, who ask how my work is going and then so patiently listen to my too-long answers.

Aaron

References

Aaron Johannes: Introduction

Quote from Adrienne Rich, "Cartographies of Silence"

David Pitonyak: The Importance of Belonging

Perske, R. (1988). *Circle of friends: People with disabilities and their friends enrich the lives of one another.* Nashville: Abingdon Press.

Pitonyak, D. (2004) Handout: The importance of belonging. Blacksburg, VA: Imagine (available online at www.dimagine.com)

Romer, M. (2002). "Two is not enough." In J. O'Brien & C. Lyle-O'Brien. *Implementing person-centered planning: Voices of experience* (121-129). Toronto: Inclusion Press.

W.C. Gaventa: Rekindling Commitment: Reflections from a Pastoral Educator Enmeshed in Direct Support Professional Workforce Development and Person Centred Supports

Cherry, B., Ashcraft, A. & Owen, D. (2007) Perceptions of job satisfaction and the regulatory environment among nurse aides and charge nurses in long-term care. *Geriatric Nursing* 28, 183–92.

DDACT2. The Developmental Disabilities Assistance and Bill of Rights Act of 2000, Public Law 106-402 – October 30, 2000; available at http://www.acf.hhs.gov/programs/add/ddact/DDACT2.html).

Demar, T. (2005) *Presentation as Part of Workshop Panel on "Developing Effective Recruitment and Retention Strategies"*. Alliance for Full Participation, Washington, DC. September, 2005. Contact: tdemar@ HeritageChristianServices.org.

Ebenstein, W. (1996) "Organizational change and the emerging partnership between direct support workers and people with disabilities." In: *Opportunities for Excellence: Supporting the Frontline Workforce* (eds. T. Jaskulski & W. Ebenstein), p. 107. The President's Committee on Mental Retardation, Administration for Children and Families, U.S. Department of Health And Human Services, Washington, DC.

Frank, B. & Dawson, S. (2000) *Healthcare workforce issues in Massachusetts. Massachusetts Health Policy Forum*. Available at: http://www.paraprofessional.org/publications/ (retrieved 5 February 2008).

Gaventa, W. (2005) "A place for all of me and all of us: rekindling the spirit in services and supports." *Mental Retardation* 43, 48–54.

Hatton, C., Emerson E., Rivers M., Mason, H., Swarbrick, R., Mason,L. *et al.* (2001) "Factors associated with intended staff turnover and job search behaviour in services for people with intellectual disability." *Journal of Intellectual Disability Research* 45, 258–70.

Hewitt, A. & Lakin, C. (2001) *Issues in the direct support workforce and their connections to the growth, sustainability, and quality of community supports.* Robert Wood Johnson Foundation, Technical Assistance Paper.

Hewitt, A., Larson, S., Lakin, C., Sauer J., O'Nell, S. & Sedlezky, L. (2004) "Role and essential competencies of the frontline supervisors of direct support professionals in community services." *Mental Retardation* 42, 122–35.

Holburn, S. (1992) "Rhetoric and realities in today's ICF/ MR: control out of control." *Mental Retardation* 30, 133–41.

Keeping the Promises (2003) *Findings and Recommendations of the 2003 Conference on National Goals, State of Knowledge, and Research Agenda for Persons with Intellectual and Developmental Disabilities.* The Arc USA, Washington, DC.

Larson, S. & Hewitt, A. (2005) *Staff Recruitment, Retention, & Training Strategies for Community Human Services Organizations.* Paul Brookes Publishing, Baltimore, MD.

Maister, D. (1997) *True Professionalism.* Free Press, New York.

Mulick, J. & Meinhold, P. (1992) "Analyzing the impact of regulations on residential ecology." *Mental Retardation* 30, 151– 63.

New Jersey Office of the Public Advocate (2007) *Recommendation on Danielle's Law.* Available at: http://www.state.nj.us/publicadvocate/home/issues/ danielleslaw.html (retrieved 5 February 2008).

O'Brien, J. & Mount, B. (2001) *Make a Difference: A Guide-book for Person-Centered Direct Support.* Inclusion Press, Toronto.

O'Brien, J. & O'Brien, C. (1994) *Assistance with integrity. The search for accountability and the lives of people with developmental disabilities. Center for Human Policy, Syracuse.* Available at: http://thechp.syr.edu/!integri.pdf (retrieved 5 February 2008).

O'Brien, J. & O'Brien, C. (1997) *Members of Each Other.* Inclusion

Press, Toronto.

O'Brien, J., O'Brien, C. & Schwartz, D. (2004) *What Can We Count on to Make and Keep People Safe? Perspectives on Creating Effective Safeguards for People with Developmental Disabilities.* Center for Human Policy, Syracuse. Available at: http://thechp.syr.edu/CountOn.pdf (retrieved 5 February 2008).

O'Brien, J. with staff from Creative Living Services (2004) "It's *How You Look at Your Work that Makes the Difference" Direct Support Workers Consider the Meaning of Their Jobs.* Responsive Systems Associates, Lithonia, GA.

Palmer, P. (1997) *The Courage to Teach: Recovering the Inner Landscape of a Teacher's Life.* Josey Bass, San Francisco, CA.

Palmer, P. (2007) *A new professional. The aims of education revisited change.* November/December. The Carnegie Foundation for the Advancement of Teaching. Available at: http://www.carnegiefoundation.org/change (retrieved 25 November 2007).

PBS. The News Hour, http://www.pbs.org., 1/23/08)

Polzer, K. (2007) *Assisted living state regulatory review.* National Center for Assisted Living. Available at: http://www.ncal.org/about/2007_reg_review.pdf (retrieved 5 February 2008).

Reinders, H. (2000) *The Future of the Disabled in Liberal Society.* University of Notre Dame Press, South Bend, IN.

Schwartz, D. (1996) *Who Cares? Rediscovering Community.* Westview Press, Denver, CO.

Shea, J. (1990) *Where's the Jello?:The Continuing Saga of One Home's Experience with the ICF/MR (Small) Program.* Allen, Shea, and Associates, Napa, CA. Email: allenshea@sbcglobal.net for copy.

Swinton, J. (2001) *Spirituality in Mental Health Care: Rediscovering a "Forgotten" Dimension.* Jessica Kingsley, London.

Taylor, S. (1992) "The paradox of regulations: a commentary." *Mental Retardation* 30, 185–90.

U.S. Department of Health and Human Services, Assistant Secretary for Planning and Evaluation, Office of Disability, Aging, and Long Term Care Policy (2006) *The Supply of Direct Support Professionals Serving Individuals with Intellectual Disabilities and Other Developmental Disabilities.* Report to Congress, Washington, DC.

Wolfensberger, W. (1977) The prophetic voice and presence of mentally retarded people in the world today. In: *The Theological Voice of Wolf Wolfensberger* (eds W. Gaventa & D. Coulter), pp. 11–48. The Haworth Press, Binghamton, NY.

Tim Stainton: Empowerment and the architecture of rights based social policy

ATTORNEY GENERAL OF BRITISH COLUMBIA (2004) *Proposal for Reform of Personal Planning and Guardianship Legislation.* Victoria. BRITISH COLUMBIA (2004) Bill 45 Community Living Authority Act. Legislative Session: 5th Session, 37th Parliament.

DAWSON, C. (2000) Independent Successes: Implementing Direct Payments. York: Joseph Rowntree Foundation.

D O H (2001) *Valuing People: A New Strategy for Learning Disability for the* 21st *Century.* Cm 5086. London: Department of Health.

DOH (2004) Direct Choices: What Councils Need to Make Direct Payments Happen for People with *Learning Disabilities.* London: Department of Health.

GLASBY, J. & LITTLECHILD, R. (2002) *SocialWork and Direct Payments.* Bristol: Policy.

Hasler, F., Campbell, J. & Zarb, J. (1999)Direct Routes to Independence: A Guide to the *Local Authority Implementation and Management of Direct Payments.* London: Joseph Rowntree Foundation/National Centre for Independent Living/Policy Studies Institute. Law Commission (1995) *Report on Mental Incapacity,* no. 231. London.

Lord Chancellor's Department (1997) *Who Decides: Making Decisions on Behalf of Mentally Incapacitated Adults.* Consultation paper. Cm 3808. London: Lord Chancellor's Department.

Lord Chancellor's Department (1999) *Making Decisions:The Government's Proposals for Making Decisions on Behalf of Mentally Incapacitated Adults.* Cm 4465. London: Lord Chancellor's Department.

Lord, J. & Hutchinson, P. (2003) "Individualized Support and Funding: Building Blocks for Capacity Building and Inclusion," *Disability & Society* 18: 71–86.

MacNicol, J. (1989) *Eugenics and the Campaign for Voluntary Sterilization in Britain between the Wars.* London: Society for the History of Medicine.

MCFD (2002) A New Vision for Community Living: A Vision of Choice and Change. Report of the Community Living Transition Steering Committee. Victoria: Ministry of Children and Family Development.

Powers, L., Sowers, J. & Singer, G. H. S. (2003) "A Cross-Disability Analysis of Person Directed Long-Term Services." MS. Portland: Centre for Self Determination.

Rosenau, N. (2002) "Individual Funding: Flavour of the Day or Sea Change?" Policy Research Briefs, paper 2. Fitzroy: Disability Foundation of Australia.

Salisbury, B., Dickey, J & Crawford, C. (1987) *Service Brokerage: Individual Empowerment and Social Service Accountability.* Downsview: G. Allan Roeher Institute.

SCRCSSP (1998) Implementing Reforms in Government Services 1998. Steering Committee for the Review of Commonwealth/State Service Provision. Canberra: AusInfo. Secretary of State for Constitutional Affairs (2003) *Draft Mental Incapacity Bill.* Cm 5859–1.

Stainton, T. (1998a) "Intellectual Disability, Difference and Oppression," in B. Lesnik (ed.) *Countering Discrimination in Social Work*. Aldershot: Ashgate/Arena.

Stainton, T. (1998b)'Rights and Rhetoric in Practice: Contradictions for Practitioners',in A. Symonds & A. Kelly (eds) The Social Construction of Community *Care,* pp. 135–44. London: Macmillan.

Stainton, T. (1994) *Autonomy and Social Policy: Rights,Mental Handicap and Community Care.* Aldershot: Avebury.

Stainton, T. & Boyce, S. (2004) "'I Have Got My Life Back': Users' Experience of Direct Payments," *Disability and Society* 19 (5): 443–54.

Thomson, M. (1998) *The Problem of Mental Deficiency: Eugenics, Democracy and Social Policy in Britain c.1870–1959.* Oxford: Clarendon.

It is our intention to give appropriate attribution wherever possible; if you notice an error, please let us know so that we can correct future editions.   Thanks.

Other resources

*Not intended to be an exhaustive list, this will give the ready
reader a sense of where to find these authors and some other
resources. A more updated list is available at
www.101friends.ca*

W.C. Gaventa, originally referenced this resource at the end
of his paper: Center for Courage and Renewal: Reconnecting
who you are with what you do. www.couragerenewal.org A
fuller sense of Bill's work and publications is at
http://rwjms.umdnj.edu/boggscenter/faculty_staff/gaventa.ht
ml

Maria Glaze and Julia Downs are long time peer parent
supporters and organizers, often affiliated with the Family
Support Institute
www.familysupportinstitutebc.com

Aaron Johannes's work is found at www.spectrumpress.ca and

www.101friends.ca   His work as a graphic facilitator and other investigations may be found at www.imagineacircle.com

Michael Kendrick's papers may be found under publications on his site www.kendrickconsulting.com

Norman Kunc and Emma Van der Kleft's work and that of Broadreach Consulting may be viewed on their site www.normemma.com

John Lord, mentioned here, has published books and many articles. See his site www.johnlord.net

Patrick McDonagh's books and papers are available in many places; try "the label game" – the original site for the interviews with Paul Young and Peter Park, currently (possibly) under revision. www.patrickmcdonagh.net

John and Connie Lyle O'Brien's many works may be found on www.inclusion.com and on other sites.

Jack Pearpoint, quoted as an epigraph, is an inspirational Canadian who has worked tirelessly for social justice through www.inclusion.com This quote is from a series of blog postings, *What Are You Skating Towards?,* organized by Al Etmanski, and found at www.aletmanski.com

David Pitonyak's work and workshops may be found online at www.dimagine.com

Judith Snow's work can be found at www.inclusion.com and at www.judithsnow.org

Tim Stainton is a much published author and active voice in community living, his work, like the work of many authors, may be searched using Google Scholar.

Susan Stanfield's work is found at www.spectrumpress.ca and www.101friends.ca

www.tash.org is one of the great curators, in several ways, of both media and leaders.

David and Faye Wetherow, although not in this anthology, have a site www.communityworks.info which features many of their articles.

Paul Young and Peter Park have been very active members of People First of Canada www.peoplefirstofcanada.ca

Spectrum Press
A DIVISION OF SPECTRUM SOCIETY

Spectrum Press is the social enterprise division of our organization, creating and distributing media by, for and about people with disabilities and those who care about them. People with developmental disabilities contribute as paid researchers, writers and in other roles, such as models and book table hosts. Our products support furthering interdependence and profits are currently focused on literacy and story-telling supports.

Spectrum Society is a not for profit organization successfully supporting adults with disabilities around greater Vancouver, British Columbia, for 25 years, in individualised, person-centred ways as they work, play and contribute in their homes, workplaces and neighbourhoods.

Spectrum Learning regularly presents workshops on a variety of topics to staff, educators, families, self advocates and mixed community groups. We also provide facilitation, planning services and supported community based research. Each year we host best practice leaders to share information from around the world.

To learn more, visit these links! www.spectrumsociety.org www.spectrumpress.ca www.101friends.ca see us on Facebook or tweet @101friendsBC or call 604-323-1433